OFFBEAT
Overnights

A GUIDE TO

THE MOST UNUSUAL PLACES TO STAY IN
CALIFORNIA

▼

Lucy Poshek

RUTLEDGE HILL PRESS
NASHVILLE, TENNESSEE

Published in Nashville, Tennessee, by Rutledge Hill Press, 211 Seventh Avenue North, Nashville, Tennessee 37219.

Distributed in Canada by H. B. Fenn and Company, Ltd., 34 Nixon Road, Bolton, Ontario L7E 1W2.

Distributed in Australia by Millennium Books, 33 Maddox Street, Alexandria NSW 2015.

Distributed in New Zealand by Tandem Press, 2 Rugby Road, Birkenhead, Auckland 10.

Distributed in the United Kingdom by Verulam Publishing, Ltd., 152a Park Street Lane, Park Street, St. Albans, Hertfordshire AL2 2AU.

Cover photographs: Top two photographs by Lucy Poshek. Bottom left photograph courtesy of Madonna Inn.

Typography by D&T/Bailey Typesetting, Inc., Nashville, Tennessee.

Photographs by Lucy Poshek, with the exception of: Madonna Inn (Cave Man Room) courtesy of Madonna Inn; Hotel Triton courtesy of Hotel Triton; Mandarin Oriental courtesy of Mandarin Oriental; Howard Creek Ranch courtesy of Howard Creek Ranch; and Fantasy Inn courtesy of Fantasy Inn.

Library of Congress Cataloging-in-Publication Data

Poshek, Lucy.
    Offbeat overnights : a guide to the most unusual places to stay in California / by Lucy Poshek.
        p.   cm.
    Includes index.
    ISBN 1-55853-390-7 (pbk.)
        1. Hotels—California—Guidebooks.   2. Bed and breakfast accommodations—California—Guidebooks.   I. Title.
    TX907.3.C2P67   1996
    647.94794'01—dc20   95-51139
                                                                          CIP

Printed in the United States of America

2 3 4 5 6 7 8 9—00 99 98 97

ACKNOWLEDGMENTS

Many thanks to my supportive family of map lovers;
to Allison Meierding, for navigating me through
twenty-five hundred miles of the journey;
to Michaeleen Crawford, for being such a good friend that
you accompanied me to Death Valley in the summer;
and to the folks at Rutledge Hill Press,
for believing in the power of the offbeat.

CALIFORNIA

The Far North

Mendocino & Lake Counties

Northern Sierras

Napa & Sonoma Counties

Southern Sierras

San Francisco Bay Area

Monterey Bay Area

Central Coast

Desert Region

Los Angeles & Vicinity

San Diego Area

CONTENTS

Introduction

Are you ready for a departure from ordinary lodgings? How about staying in a converted lighthouse, caboose, or water tower? Searching for an unforgettable bed? Try sleeping in a Roman chariot or a fifties Cadillac convertible complete with its own drive-in movie screen. Romance? How about a waterfall shower for two? Seclusion? There's a quiet monastery waiting just for you.

Offbeat Overnights contains frank, often irreverent reviews of more than two hundred unique lodgings in every corner of California. Destinations range from paddle wheelers to enchanted treehouses to New Age spas. Some places are so rustic or remote that you can only reach them by boat; others are ultra-modern, cutting-edge city hotels. They range from cheap hostels to $6,000-a-night suites, running the gamut from mildly novel to wildly outlandish. All share the desirable qualities of character, spirit, and originality.

Not all lodgings scream out their uniqueness right away. They might appear quite unremarkable from the outside, only to reveal delightful little surprises inside. In Mendocino, for example, the Brewery Gulch Inn looks innocuous enough—pretty gardens and simple guest rooms. But in place of the usual evening mint on the nightstand is a little burlap bag with a note that says, "For your chicken-feeding pleasure." Sure enough, tucked behind the inn is a veritable chicken Hilton—an elaborate, multilevel coop with cut-glass windows, an undulating roof, and the happiest chickens you ever saw.

Little gems like that bag of chicken feed first inspired me to write this book. While reviewing hundreds of accommodations for other guidebooks, I began searching for any little feature that made a place stand out, like an unconventional bed, romantic bathtub, or novel amenity. Among a sea of conformity in the hostelry business, I found mischievous signs of rebellion. I also discovered that those unique touches are what guests savor the most.

People are traveling more than ever now, and their tastes are growing more adventurous. Most of us have already tried the weekend at a Hallmark-type bed and breakfast, the generic ski condo, or the institutional business hotel. Today we're looking for more than just a place to sleep; we want a one-of-a-kind, exciting experience in exchange for our hard-earned dollar; a travel fantasy fulfilled. *Offbeat Overnights* covers just about every fantasy in the book.

To ensure that this guide would be as comprehensive and accurate as possible, I logged over ten thousand miles personally visiting over five hundred establishments. From this, I narrowed my list down to the two hundred most extraordinary places. My main criteria was this: Did the lodging or its surroundings or its amenities or even one room offer something singularly special? If so, I was willing to overlook a few foibles for the sake of originality. But any place that wasn't clean, friendly, or unusual enough was simply eliminated.

Offbeat Overnights travels up the west coast of California, then down its eastern length. Within each region the towns are arranged alphabetically. If you're looking for something specific, such as white-water ballooning, llamas, or French chateaux, check the Offbeat Interest Index in the back of the book. The more playful your interests are, the more likely it is that you will find them here. The index is like a looking-glass version of the yellow pages—if you can't find it, then it's probably too boring.

Offbeat Overnights is dedicated to those of you with a taste for the uncommon. I also salute those creative proprietors and innkeepers who dared to push their establishments past the ordinary. In a world of often increasing conformity, I admire your spirit.

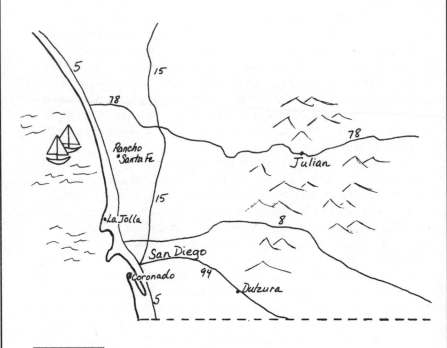

1 SAN DIEGO AREA

Coronado Victorian House

When Bonni Marie Kinosian, a dance teacher, was denied permission to turn her restored Victorian home into a bed and breakfast, she cleverly skirted the issue by getting a special-use permit: Guests buying an "intensive dance package" could spend the night. Thus was born the concept of D & D—Dance and Doze—at the Coronado Victorian House.

Included with your room and breakfast is one dance or exercise lesson. What kind of dance? Anything you wish to learn—tap, jitterbug, two-step, tango, even belly dancing. Waltzes and fox trots are Bonni Marie's most frequent requests. She has also choreographed many first dances for soon-to-be brides and grooms. Bonni Marie claims she can cure anyone of two left feet. Give her an hour in the dance studio and you'll learn the basics of at least one dance. She also teaches stretch and exercise classes, often leading her guests on early morning fitness walks to the beach.

A flamboyant, warm-hearted, health-conscious "dance-keeper," Bonni Marie loves to expound on proper breathing, posture, diet, and energy levels. She says all of her guests take away something they can use for the rest of their lives. I found myself sitting up straighter by the minute while she chatted away and plied me with her homemade Lebanese-Armenian goodies—the house specialty. Ask for her ethnic breakfast and you might be served yogurt, baklava, stuffed grape leaves, and fresh-baked Armenian bread. She also puts together Middle Eastern picnic baskets upon request.

The guest rooms are named after famous dancers, such as Balanchine, Pavlova, and Fred and Ginger. They're all on the small side, but some, like the Baryshnikov Room, compensate with unusually high antique beds. You can climb the steps of the bed or execute a ballet leap.

Only a block away is downtown Coronado, which still has a Southern California-of-the-fifties' feel. It's a neat town for strolling.

CORONADO VICTORIAN HOUSE

Telephone:	**(619) 435-2200**
Address:	**1000 Eighth Street, Coronado 92118**
Rates:	**$200 to $450, including full breakfast and dance or fitness lesson**
Directions:	**From I-5, cross the Coronado Bay Bridge to Orange Avenue and turn left, then right on Eighth Street.**

Hotel Del Coronado

Not only is the Hotel Del Coronado the largest beach resort on the Pacific Coast, it's also one of the world's biggest wooden structures. With its red conical towers (the roof is covered with two million red shingles), multiple gables, and rotundas, the legendary Victorian landmark has become synonymous with Coronado Island, a long peninsula in San Diego Bay. Over the past century the "Hotel Del" has attracted princes, presidents, and moviemakers. Frank L. Baum used it as the inspiration for the Emerald City when he wrote part of *The Wizard of Oz* here. And it was here, not Florida, where Marilyn Monroe cavorted with Tony Curtis and Jack Lemmon for the filming of *Some Like It Hot*.

The Hotel Del remains remarkable in part because of its classic Victorian resort architecture. The grand old lobby is full of warm oak and exposed beamed ceilings, with an old-fashioned birdcage elevator still in operation. Guests dine in the Crown Room, where the thirty-foot pine ceiling is held together solely with wooden pegs—there are no nails or interior supports in the entire ceiling.

Although a modern wing has been added, the older, more unique guest quarters in the Victorian building continue to merit special attention. One of the best choices is the Turret Room, with its quirky layout. All rooms have a special television channel featuring movies filmed at the hotel.

Even if you don't stay at the Hotel Del, you should try to visit at Christmastime, when the entire building is trimmed with white lights. A giant tree, decorated in a different theme every year, towers to the lofty ceiling of the lobby. A wonderful Christmas dinner is served in the Crown Room, while carolers sing from the balcony.

HOTEL DEL CORONADO

Telephone: **(800) HOTEL DEL; (619) 522-8000; fax (619) 522-8262**
Address: **1500 Orange Avenue, Coronado 92118**
Rates: **$169 to $389 in the Victorian building**
Directions: **From I-5, take Coronado Bay Bridge (SR-75) to Orange Avenue and turn left.**

DULZURA

Brookside Farm Bed & Breakfast Inn

Knowing Brookside Farm was only ten miles from the Mexican border, I always pictured it as a flat, dry locale with tumbleweeds rolling by. Granted, this is a desert region, but it's by no means flat or boring. The rolling hills are full of texture, especially in the spring. And the colorful grounds of Brookside Farm are astonishingly lush. The terraced lawns bordering the main house and extending down to the stream are an almost neon green. Flowers are everywhere. The four acres of grounds are dotted with aviaries of cooing doves and chirping parakeets. A hot tub sits under a leafy grape arbor. If this is the desert, you could have fooled me.

The homey, guest rooms with various themes tend to be dimly lit, but they're decorated with an abundance of knickknacks and memorabilia. Four rooms are in the twenties farmhouse, where happily cluttered living and dining rooms are found. There are also two private cottages, one perched right at the creek's

Flowers abound at the Brookside Farm Bed & Breakfast.

edge. It's rustic in an Old West way with authentic, straw-plastered walls, pine floors, and a wood-burning stove.

The most engaging guest quarters are in a converted barrel-roofed stone barn adjacent to the farmhouse. Two romantic upstairs suites with arched ceilings highlight the barn. One of the suites, A Room With a View, has a private balcony and double-sided fireplace. The other, Jennie's Room, overlooks the rose garden and is furnished in Victoriana, with a bathtub near the bedroom fireplace. Another favorite is Peter Rabbit's House, a cheery, country-style room with a wood-burning stove and screened porch that faces the creek and the morning sunrise. The decor is based on Beatrix Potter's stories. Bunnies are constantly multiplying here. Stuffed rabbits, framed prints of rabbits, rabbit wallpaper, ceramic rabbits—they're even in the chandelier if you look closely.

Brookside Farm is a place to come and get away from everything. There's no real town nearby. Badminton and horse-shoes are the most exciting activity of the day. And because local restaurants are almost nonexistent, most weekend guests wind up having dinner here. Innkeeper Edd Guishard, a casual, down-home kind of guy, was at one time in the restaurant business and is quite skilled in the kitchen. His wife, Sally, does all the baking. Many of the ingredients come straight from the Guishards' herb and vegetable garden, fruit orchard, berry patch, and vineyard. The Guishards also keep a collection of livestock, including peacocks, goats, guinea fowl, pigs, and a beautiful but mean-as-all-get-out silver pheasant named Elvis.

BROOKSIDE FARM BED & BREAKFAST INN

Telephone: **(619) 468-3043**
Address: **1373 Marron Valley Road, Dulzura 92017**
Rates: **$75 to $115, including full breakfast; dinners available on weekends**
Directions: **From San Diego, follow SR-94 to Dulzura and turn right on Marron Valley Road.**

JULIAN

Shadow Mountain Ranch

Jim and Loretta Ketcherside have fulfilled their most whimsical fantasies at the Shadow Mountain Ranch outside Julian. Among the more novel accommodations on their eight wooded acres are the Tree House, Enchanted Cottage, and Gnome Home.

The Gnome Home looks like a giant mushroom sprouting out of the ground among the pines. There are no straight lines—you enter via a circular tunnel into a round room crowned by an octagonal skylight. Gnome figurines and books are everywhere. The wizened little men are even carved into the hand-crafted bed and furnishings. Hidden around the corner is a rustic rock waterfall shower. It doesn't take much imagination to see the hobbit, Bilbo Baggins, there in the corner.

The Tree House was built within the upper arms of a giant oak. But the name sounds more intriguing than the actual structure. An easy-to-climb stairway leads from the deck of the main house up to a rather narrow, plain room. To take a shower,

The Shadow Mountain Ranch's Gnome Home resembles a giant mushroom.

you have to walk outside and back down the stairs. Most guests prefer the cozy, Hansel-and-Gretel-style Enchanted Cottage with its wood stove and inviting window seat.

All six rooms and cottages are cheerful and comforting, with eccentricities hidden everywhere. Even the Pine Room, conventional in appearance, conceals a secret passageway that leads directly to the hot tub. The whole setting is quite sylvan, which is out of character for Southern California. A short stroll down the hill through the cow pasture leads you to a fish pond and mill house which offers a little bed tucked inside for serious daydreamers.

SHADOW MOUNTAIN RANCH

Telephone: **(619) 765-0323**
Address: **2771 Frisius Road, Box 791, Julian 92036**
Rates: **$80 to $100, including afternoon tea and full breakfast (in the apple orchard, weather permitting)**
Directions: **From SR-78 east, just before Julian, turn right on Pine Hills Road, then left on Frisius Road.**

Shadow Mountain's Enchanted Cottage would be home to Hansel and Gretel.

LeeLin Wikiup

The LeeLin Wikiup, a small bed and breakfast on the wooded out-skirts of Julian, also accommodates four pet llamas. Owner Linda Stanley has trained "the boys" to carry packs so they can accompany guests on picnic treks. Their names—Vortex ("Tex"), Wellington, Jester, and the Reverend Mr. Black—are deliberately un-Peruvian, for these boys are Southern California-born and raised.

As we entered their corral to herd up two of them for a photo, Linda told me there are more than one hundred llama ranches in Southern California alone.

LeeLin Wikiup owner Linda Stanley has pet llamas for friends.

"Stand at the entrance, hold out your arms, and don't move, so they'll think you're a barrier," she said, trying to corner and harness one.

Suddenly, they all were galloping straight toward me, looking a lot bigger than I expected. Of course, without hesitation I jumped out of the way.

Apparently, llamas are becoming the pack animal of the future. They're easier on the terrain than mules because they have soft hooves, small pellets, and a gentle nature—once harnessed, that is. These boys also do their community service each Christmas by standing in as camels for Julian's annual nativity scene.

LEELIN WIKIUP

Telephone: **(800) 6-WIKIUP; (619) 765-1890**
Address: **1645 Whispering Pines Drive, P.O. Box 2363, Julian 92036**
Rates: **$98 to $115, including full breakfast; $55 per person for half-day llama treks**
Directions: **East of Julian on SR-78, turn right at the second Whispering Pines Drive sign. Look for the "llama crossing" sign in the left-hand driveway.**

LA JOLLA

Hyatt Regency La Jolla

Visitors either love the architecture of the Hyatt Regency La Jolla or hate it, but no one certainly feels indifferent about it. Designed by progressive architect Michael Graves, the postmodern hotel rises above a complex of eye-catching structures near the San Diego Freeway. The whole business complex is called Aventine, after one of the seven hills of Rome. Personally, I love it, but it doesn't look like any hill in Rome to me.

The interior of the Hyatt provokes an equal amount of controversy. One guidebook calls it "mausoleum moderne," which implies cold, stark public halls with half-dead business people strewn about.

Actually, the interior is rich with texture and well worth seeing if you're at all interested in design. Graves's unique blending of the neoclassic, postmodern, and Mediterranean—much imitated in a glut of far-too-pink buildings throughout Southern California—is found in abundance here. In the bar (Michael's) the walls are hand-painted in textured earth tones and decorated with ancient Roman bas-reliefs. In contrast to this classic backdrop are high-tech pool tables, black leather couches, and futuristic, black-lacquered lamps. Somehow, it all works together marvelously.

Stroll the grounds and you'll notice some peculiar parallels—such as the sixteen columns in the entry lobby reflected by sixteen palm trees in the opposite courtyard; or the square patterns throughout the public and guest rooms that match the square windows outside. Every pillar, lamp, and tree has been placed with careful deliberation. The pillars crop up again out by the swimming pool, made especially alluring by a row of glamorous cabanas.

As for those aforementioned "half-dead business people," most of them are very much alive and working out in the Sporting Club, a sleek, three-level health spa near the pool. Almost every imaginable exercise machine—cross-country skiing, rowing, walking, cycling, stair master—is here in multiples. And, unlike most hotel gyms, these state-of-the-art objects of torture are actually being used. Perhaps it's all an extension of Graves's Roman motif—modern-day gladiators pumping themselves up for a day of head-bashing at the conference tables.

HYATT REGENCY LA JOLLA

Telephone: **(800) 233-1234; (619) 552-1234; fax (619) 552-6066**
Address: **3777 La Jolla Village Drive, San Diego 92122**
Rates: **$153 to $178, single; $178 to $203, double; concierge floor rooms include continental breakfast and evening hors d'oeuvres**
Directions: **From I-5, exit La Jolla Village Drive.**

RANCHO SANTA FE

The Inn at Rancho Santa Fe

The Inn at Rancho Santa Fe is early California at its best. The low, Spanish-style buildings are surrounded by an expansive lawn and graceful rows of towering eucalyptus trees. The great lounge is much as it was in the old days, with wood floors, high beamed ceilings, and a massive fireplace. Ladies love to come here and lunch in the outdoor patio or library. The whole inn embodies an understated patrician air.

Built in 1923, the inn has been run by the same family for three generations. Originally, the property was owned by the Santa Fe Railroad—they were the ones who imported and planted all the eucalyptus in the mistaken belief that the trees would make good railroad ties. The happy results of their failure have proliferated throughout the town.

THE INN AT RANCHO SANTA FE

Telephone: **(800) 654-2928; (619) 756-1131; fax (619) 759-1604**
Address: **P.O. Box 869, Rancho Santa Fe 92067**
Rates: **$85 to $485**
Directions: **in downtown Rancho Santa Fe, on Linea del Cielo.**

SAN DIEGO

San Diego Princess

Aside from the Hotel Del Coronado, the most remarkable resort in the San Diego area is the San Diego Princess. Formerly known as Vacation Village, the Princess is spread over a forty-four-acre island in the heart of Mission Bay.

The Princess is ringed by a mile-long circle of white beach. Within this framework, roads and paths meander mazelike from cottage to cottage, through impeccably landscaped grounds, lagoons, fish ponds, and waterfalls. A spindly observation tower rises from the heart of the resort, overlooking all of San Diego.

When it comes to activities, the Princess is exhaustingly self-sufficient. There's a fancy eighteen-hole putting green, boat rentals from a private marina, a jogging course, bicycle and quadricycle rentals, a botanical walk, tennis, massage, aerobics, swimming, summer camps for children, shuffleboard, a video game room, fitness center, live music in the bar and grill, and duck feeding. (They sell duck food in the gift shop.) On top of all this, Sea World is just across the bridge.

The most requested accommodations are the studio and one-bedroom suites with bay views. From some of these rooms you can see the water from your bed. The one-bedroom suites have kitchens and a living room couch that folds out into two twin beds—a clever solution for kids who don't like sleeping together. And if you really need some breathing space, there's a 4,200-square-foot presidential suite—but you don't want to know how much that costs. (Okay—it's $2,250 a night.)

One of the nicest things about the Princess is that it appeals equally well to families, romantic couples, and business people. It's kid-friendly and even pet-friendly—dogs and cats are also welcome—yet the sprawling, tropical layout keeps the atmosphere serene. It manages to be informal yet lovely at the same time. The staff is quite accommodating; if you want, you can even have a barbecue on your patio. So pack up your kids, cat, hibachi, and bring them all down.

SAN DIEGO PRINCESS

Telephone: **(800) 344-2626; (619) 274-4630**
Address: **1404 West Vacation Road, San Diego 92109**
Rates: **$130 to $2,250. Pets welcome.**
Directions: **From I-5, exit Sea World Drive and head west; turn right at Sports Arena Boulevard (which becomes Ingraham Street) and cross bridge to Vacation Isle.**

The Horton Grand

The Horton Grand is an odd bird in San Diego's historic Gaslamp Quarter. In 1986, three nineteenth-century hotels were dismantled and reassembled at this downtown site, resulting in a new "old" hotel with a somewhat eclectic decor. The central courtyard, with its white wicker chairs and birds twittering in their cages, is reminiscent of New Orleans, whereas the guest rooms are distinctly Victorian. The Viennese-style Palace Bar—a high-ceilinged, sumptuously muraled room—is the setting for both English high tea in the afternoon and international jazz in the evenings.

Although the Horton Grand walks a fine line between charming and slightly cheesy, an admirable attempt has been made to re-create a romantic, old-fashioned setting for guests. Each guest room (those with balconies facing the courtyard seem most tranquil) has a gas-burning fireplace, with the television cleverly hidden behind a mirror above the mantle. The bellman is dressed in turn-of-the-century clothing. Now and then a horse-drawn carriage or antique car stops at the front steps for a tour around the Gaslamp Quarter.

Apparently, the atmosphere is nostalgic enough to draw some otherworldly lodgers, too. Room 309, for example, is allegedly haunted by a ghost named Roger who has a naughty habit of turning the lights on and off, vibrating the beds, and moving pictures around. According to investigating psychics, Roger was a gambler from the 1800s who was shot by an associate while hiding inside the armoire of a different hotel. No one seems to know how he got here, but Roger has created enough havoc in Room 309 to prompt several shaken guests to check out in the middle of the night complaining of an unusual presence. On similar occasions, the chambermaids have refused to clean the room. Despite these incidents, Room 309 is always booked solid. If you can't get this room, don't despair: These same psychics claim there are ghosts all over the hotel—"dancing, wandering, and just hanging out."

THE HORTON GRAND

Telephone: **(800) HERITAGE; (619) 544-1886; fax (619) 239-3823**
Address: **311 Island Avenue, San Diego 92101**
Rates: **$139 to $218**
Directions: **From I-5 south, exit at Front Street, proceed south and turn left on Broadway; turn right on Fourth Avenue, then right on Island Avenue.**

LITTLE NOVELTY: Attention music buffs: Every April through October, **Humphrey's Half Moon Inn** hosts a "Concert by the Bay" series of jazz and pop music. Among their entertainers in past years—Ray Charles, Kenny G, Harry Belafonte, Smokey Robinson, and George Benson. The outdoor stage is surrounded by the hotel, so you can enjoy live music right from your room. The Polynesian-style hotel is next to the yacht harbor on Shelter Island. For more information, call (800) 345-9995 or (619) 224-3411.

At Crystal Pier Hotel, the views are terrific in any direction.

Crystal Pier Hotel

Where can you sleep over the water without being on a boat? At the Crystal Pier Hotel, where the waves crash right under your cottage out on the pier.

The blue and white cottages run halfway down both sides of Crystal Pier in Pacific Beach. Regardless of which side you choose, the views are terrific, with long stretches of sandy beach in either direction. Each cottage has a deck facing the sea.

One decision needs to be made here—whether to stay in one of the thirties cottages or splurge on one of the newer, bigger cottages farther out on the pier. The older units are slightly frayed and funky with one long communal deck; the six new cottages are fresher, have much nicer kitchenettes, and boast private decks. In winter, the new units are nearly twice the price of the old ones.

The most novel part of staying on Crystal Pier is the sound of the waves underneath you. Despite the fact that Pacific

Beach is congested in the summer and its boardwalk is a constant parade, the pier itself is surprisingly quiet and peaceful. Nothing but squawking sea gulls disturb the soothing sound of the waves.

CRYSTAL PIER HOTEL

Telephone: **(800) 748-5894; (619) 483-6983**
Address: **4500 Ocean Boulevard, San Diego 92109**
Rates: **$85-180. Two-night minimum in winter, three nights in summer (but if you drop by that day and space is available, they'll sometimes waive the requirement)**
Directions: **From I-5 south, exit at Garnet Avenue and head for the ocean. Guests can drive their cars down the pier and park directly in front of their cottage.**

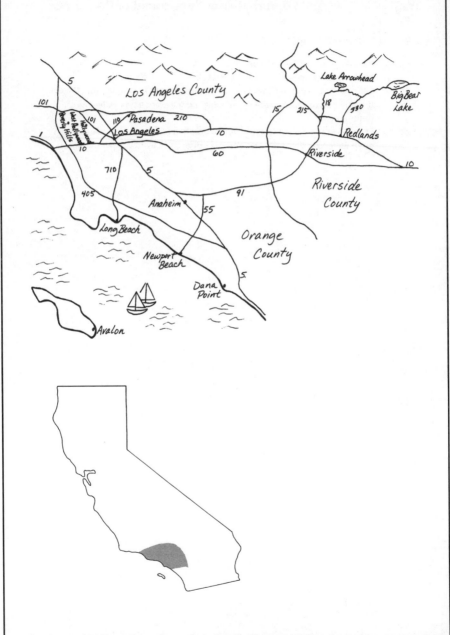

2 LOS ANGELES and VICINITY

Disneyland Hotel

I balked at including the Disneyland Hotel here because its sixties high-rises and guest rooms are devoid of character. Looks can be deceiving. This hotel offers many other one-of-a-kind features that place it in a league of its own. Where else, for instance, can you be delivered to your hotel by a monorail? Where else can you use "Disney dollars" to pay for your food, park admission, and merchandise? (Women will be pleased to see that Minnie's face rates a ten-dollar bill while Mickey is stuck on a one-dollar bill.) And at what other hotel can you watch fireworks and a spectacular water display right from your room?

The centerpiece of this sixty-acre resort is its enormous, man-made marina, complete with paddleboats, waterfalls, koi ponds, and a white beach. The waterfalls are like a Disney ride themselves; you can stroll right underneath them. In the morning and evening, management offers a public fish feeding (which probably explains why the koi are so incredibly fat). And later in the evening is Fantasy Waters—the highlight of staying here. This dazzling after-dusk show features dancing fountains with lights, music, the works. Every night during the summer season, the park puts on a spectacular fireworks display.

The marina at any hour is a show in itself, with all the lakeside games (remote-controlled tugboats, race cars, etc.) and crowds of people passing by, wearing and carrying the most outrageous Disney memorabilia.

Of course, kids love the Disneyland Hotel. There's no end to things for them to do. Take them to breakfast at Goofy's

Kitchen, the hotel's coffee shop, where they will meet Aladdin, Pinocchio, and, yes, Goofy.

If you're interested in a room with any semblance of character, ask for the Oriental Garden section. Set off to one corner, these two-story buildings overlook lovely, manicured Japanese gardens. With private balconies and enclosed patios, the rooms are a bit more intimate than those in the three uncomely high-rises that dominate the grounds.

DISNEYLAND HOTEL

Telephone:	**(714) 956-MICKEY; (714) 956-6425; fax (714) 956-6582**
Address:	**1150 West Cerritos Avenue, Anaheim 92802**
Rates:	**$150 to $2,000**
Directions:	**From I-5 south, exit at Ball Road and turn right. From I-5 north, exit at Katella Avenue and head east.**

AVALON, CATALINA ISLAND

The Inn on Mt. Ada

Staying at the Inn on Mt. Ada is like having your own private island villa. Situated high above crescent-shaped Avalon Harbor, this Georgian colonial mansion has long been an aristocratic landmark of Catalina Island.

The island's owner at the time, chewing gum tycoon William Wrigley, Jr., built the mansion in 1921 as a summer home for his wife Ada. Known as the "West Coast White House," the mansion hosted such notable visitors as Calvin Coolidge and the Duke of Windsor. Because Wrigley used the island as the spring training site for his Chicago Cubs baseball team, he could look down on their practice field from his office window. If he wasn't pleased with their performance, he sent a messenger down the mountain bearing bad news.

When the historic building was leased from the University of Southern California to be converted to an inn in 1985, the mansion underwent a million-dollar restoration. They kept the moldings, panelwork, and beveled windows intact, but replaced

Staying at the Inn on Mt. Ada is like having your own private island villa.

the dark twenties decor with light, elegant furnishings. Mr. and Mrs. Wrigley's former bedrooms have been turned into graceful suites. The porcelain bathtubs remain, although they no longer draw heated sea water. In addition to six guest rooms (which have glorious ocean views), there's a spacious living room, wicker-filled sun porch, white-columned terrace with telescope, and dining room. All meals are included, so you never have to set foot outside the mansion. If you do decide to make the steep descent into town, you're handed the keys to a complimentary golf cart to get around the island.

Because of its mountaintop seclusion and the fact that the public is allowed entry only by appointment, the inn has an ultra-private quality. The innkeepers live in separate quarters on the grounds, so guests have free reign of the mansion at night. It's odd to see twinkling lights in the distance and realize you're facing the coast of Southern California. Locals call it "the mainland," as if it were another state.

THE INN ON MT. ADA

Telephone: **(310) 510-2030**
Address: **1 Wrigley Road, P.O. Box 2560, Avalon, Catalina Island 90704**
Rates: **$340 to $620, including all meals**
Directions: **Upon disembarking from the ferry in Avalon, guests are picked up by a private van.**

BEVERLY HILLS

The Beverly Prescott Hotel

Formerly known as the Beverly Hillcrest, the Prescott has the same whimsical charm of the Hotel Triton in San Francisco—indeed, they were both designed by the same company—with its loopy, fantasy furnishings and avant-garde touches. Whereas the Triton is done in cool colors, the Beverly Prescott glows with warmth. The guest rooms, all of which have balconies overlooking Beverly Hills, are painted in exaggerated checks or stripes, with trompe l'oeil side tables and floral pillows. In the living room, a soft cranberry velvet sofa contrasts playfully with yellow hassocks, spindly coffee tables, and triangular chairs. Beaded masks on the fireplace mantle gaze across to fat stone columns that are crowned by mounds of moss. The quirky decor is stylish and visually stimulating—a breath of fresh new life in what was once a stodgy old hotel.

There's even a Jerry Garcia Suite here, just like at the Triton. Not only does it feature his custom-designed fabrics, but the CD player comes stocked with all of his Grateful Dead recordings.

THE BEVERLY PRESCOTT HOTEL

Telephone: **(800) 421-3212; (310) 277-2800; fax (310) 203-9537**
Address: **1224 South Beverwil Drive, P.O. Box 3065, Beverly Hills 90035**
Rates: **$185 to $700**
Directions: **at Beverwil and Rodeo Drive.**

The Beverly Hills Hotel

Perhaps no other establishment captures the essence of old movie-star glamour like the Beverly Hills Hotel. Wherever you look there's soft salmon pink, gold leaf, and palm trees—the quint-essential symbols of Hollywood. Movers and shakers still meet in the Polo Lounge for early morning power breakfasts just as they did in the forties, while beautiful people with too-perfect faces stroll out to the pool in white terry robes and expensive sunglasses.

The only thing that has changed at this timeless hotel is the guests, who are more spoiled than ever. But hey, that's okay, because here at the "Pink Palace" you can get anything you want, no matter how eccentric the request. When frequent guest Walter Annenberg complained about the lack of privacy around the hotel's swimming pool, they built him a four-bedroom bungalow with his own private lap pool. When Howard Hughes (who always booked four bungalows—two to use as decoys) demanded roast beef sandwiches be hidden for him in a tree in the garden, no one batted an eye. If a VIP guest wants to set up a permanent personal phone and fax line at the hotel, he's got it. Their "we-never-say-no" policy and protection of the guests' privacy has brought the hotel a fiercely loyal clientele. The bungalows are set up like private residences since many people end up staying for quite a while.

Among the other unique amenities here: the walk-in closets have little his-and-hers terry robes for children; many suites and bungalows feature baby grand pianos; hidden in the armoires are hi-tech sound systems; every room comes equipped with a fax machine and four phone lines (including a direct pri-vate one), plus butler service buttons, Ralph Lauren linens, and guest-chosen newspaper delivery; the bath toiletries are prettily presented in a hat box; and the bungalow kitchens have a separate entry door for staff members to deliver candlelight room service or cook dinner without disturbing guests. The presidential suite has a full-scale industrial kitchen, his-and-hers closets, marble Jacuzzi baths, and cut-crystal bath accessories. Out by the Olympic-sized swimming pool, guests are refreshed with chilled towels and afternoon sorbets.

The Pink Palace was given a $100 million facelift in 1992. Its signature pink color, bell towers, undulating lines, and sprawling twelve acres of grounds remain much as they were in their golden days, only better. One corner that hasn't changed a bit is the downstairs Fountain Coffee Shop, a favorite burger and soda haunt of celebrities. It still has its pink bar stools, homemade ice creams, and authentic twenties' feel.

THE BEVERLY HILLS HOTEL

Telephone: **(800) 283-8885; (310) 276-2251; fax (310) 281-2905**
Address: **Sunset Boulevard, Beverly Hills 90210**
Rates: **$275 to $3,000**
Directions: **on Sunset Boulevard, between Coldwater Canyon and Benedict Canyon Drive.**

BIG BEAR LAKE

The Knickerbocker Mansion

This isn't one of those Hallmark-like bed and breakfasts found all over Big Bear and Lake Arrowhead. The Knickerbocker Mansion is a rambling, old twenties mountain home handcrafted entirely from logs. The wood paneling, ceilings, and wonderful, split-log staircase—they just don't make 'em like this anymore.

Although it was built in the twenties, the whole mansion has more of a nostalgic, forties feel to it. Guests are greeted by Wiley, the resident dog (who seems to have a perpetual smile on his face) and the sound of big band music playing in the living room. The living room is comfortably cluttered with memorabilia—an old Victrola, a collection of pipes, and cushy velvet sofas. A double-sided stone fireplace faces both the living room and a sunny breakfast room. Old rockers sit exactly as they've sat for seventy years on the long covered porches. The decor isn't perfectly coordinated (it wouldn't have been in the forties either), but it is very comfortable mountain lodging. And it has real character.

Some guest quarters are in a separate carriage house up the hill, but my favorite rooms are in the main house: Calico, because of its private access to the porch, and Uncle Will's Room, named after the owner's distant uncle, Will Rogers. Uncle Will's Room is rustically furnished in an Old West theme, complete with saddle, spurs, and Indian relics. The Penthouse fills the entire third floor, which was once the attic. An incredibly wide room, with separate bed nooks flanking either side of the main bed, it's dominated by a big-screen TV—a bit incongruous for a mountain retreat like this.

After a hearty breakfast, wander out to a hammock under the pines. Take peanuts with you—the squirrels will come tugging at your pants.

THE KNICKERBOCKER MANSION

Telephone: (800) 785-5535; (909) 866-8221
Address: 869 South Knickerbocker Road, P.O. Box 3661, Big Bear Lake 92315
Rates: $75 to $225, including breakfast
Directions: Entering Big Bear Lake from SR-18 east, turn right on Knickerbocker Road.

Castle Wood Cottages

Storybook themes blend delightfully with adult luxuries at Castle Wood Cottages in Big Bear. These ten, cute-as-a-button cottages look like they're transported from Disneyland. Each theme is carried to the hilt. King Arthur's Cabin, for instance, is decorated like a chamber in a dark castle, with fake castle stone, velvet and gold drapes, stained glass, a hand-carved bed, and coat of arms over the fireplace. Lest you think this is just for kids, however, there's also a double Jacuzzi in front of the fireplace. And if you really want to get kinky, King Arthur and Guinevere costumes hang suggestively on the wall.

Among the most engaging cottages are Robin and Marian's Suite (swathed in hunter green and burgundy, with a lacy half-canopy bed), Heidi's Cabin (stone and wood walls, flower boxes), and Gone With the Wind (a miniature, two-story southern mansion complete with Vivien Leigh's portrait over the mantle). These cottages all have whirlpool tubs facing the fireplaces, VCRs, and theme costumes. Gone With the Wind also features a fifty-two-inch big screen television with surround sound. Guess what video goes with it?

My personal favorite is the Captain's Quarters. The whole spacious, skylit cabin is paneled in oak like the inside of a ship. Next to the whirlpool tub is a treasure chest brimming with faux gold and jewels. The fireplace is decorated with a model ship and skull. Pirate maps are embossed on the wet bar, where there is also a lantern and pirate figurines. Open the hatch on the floor and it triggers the recorded sound of a diabolical voice and yo-ho-ho music. In the hatch are the skeletal remains of a pirate.

The cottages are centered around a tidy playground with a duck pond, children's playhouse, see-saw, Ping-Pong table, barbecue, and picnic table, all painted a cheerful violet and sky blue. Like Disneyland, every little functional object is disguised. Even the trash can is hidden in a fake wishing well. This is a great place for both kids and adults.

CASTLE WOOD COTTAGES

Telephone: **(909) 866-2720**
Address: **547 Main Street, P.O. Box 1746, Big Bear Lake 92315**
Rates: **$39 to $219**
Directions: **Entering Big Bear Lake from SR-18 east, turn right on Main Street.**

DANA POINT

The Ritz-Carlton Laguna Niguel

Everyone knows how luxurious Ritz-Carltons are, and the Ritz-Carlton Laguna Niguel is no exception. Its elegant interior of museum-quality artwork and antiques is matched only by its spectacular setting on a bluff above the ocean. And the service is incredible. I was at a wedding here once. While walking from the ceremony to the reception, one of my friends lost a button from her jacket. A staff member suddenly appeared out of nowhere, whisked the jacket away, and reappeared five minutes later with the button replaced. And we weren't even staying there.

Because the Ritz is just down the road from my home, I find any excuse to get dressed up and go there as often as possible.

An afternoon tea in the wood-paneled library has become a yearly Easter Day ritual. My mother loves the elaborate flower arrangements. For kids, there are teddy bear teas, puppet shows, and tidepool explorations. Adults can take cooking classes and garden tours.

But my favorite time of the year to visit the Ritz is at Christmas, when the hotel turns into a veritable wonderland. The trees lining the driveway are covered with no less than 350,000 tiny white lights. Inside, the scene is equally breathtaking—a Christmas tree with ornaments from all over the world, sumptuous decorations, and strolling carolers. And downstairs is the most incredible gingerbread house you'll ever see. Every year, five engineers spend a hundred hours designing this ten-foot house. It takes fifteen pastry chefs two weeks to make it. They use three hundred pounds of flour, five hundred eggs, ten pounds of spices, and thirty pounds of candy. The icing requires another two hundred pounds of powdered sugar and twenty quarts of egg whites. Don't try this at home, folks.

THE RITZ-CARLTON LAGUNA NIGUEL

Telephone:	**(800) 241-3333; (714) 240-2000; fax (714) 240-0829**
Address:	**33533 Ritz-Carlton Drive, Dana Point 92629**
Rates:	**$215 to $475**
Directions:	**on Highway 1, just north of Dana Point.**

HOLLYWOOD

Hollywood Roosevelt Hotel

Apparently, the Hollywood Roosevelt Hotel is filled with spirit in more ways than one. Since its reopening in 1985, the hotel has had so many ghostly occurrences, the director of security is keeping a log of strange events. In the Blossom Room, where the first Academy Awards ceremony was held in 1929, a mysterious thirty-inch "cold spot" was discovered. It's still there. The mirror in the downstairs elevator landing is notorious, not only because it belonged to Marilyn Monroe, but because a guest once saw the reflection of a blonde woman in it—even though no one was there. Maids have complained of a strange presence in Room 928 where Montgomery Clift lived for several months. Among other occurrences—lights turned on and the sounds of electric typewriters were heard in unoccupied, locked rooms; and a man in a white suit, seen by three different people on two different days, walked through a door and vanished. One day, five people watched and listened in disbelief to sounds of metal scraping on the concrete floor of an unfinished, empty penthouse.

Located across from Mann's Chinese Theatre, the 1927 hotel has seen a lot of movie history. The Spanish colonial lobby, with its elaborate hand-painted ceiling and tile floors, is steeped in twenties and thirties ambiance, but the rest of the hotel could use a jump start.

HOLLYWOOD ROOSEVELT HOTEL

Telephone: **(800) 950-7667; (213) 466-7000; fax (213) 469-7006**
Address: **7000 Hollywood Boulevard, Hollywood 90028**
Rates: **$109 to $1,500**
Directions: **on Hollywood Boulevard, between Highland and La Brea Avenues.**

Chateau Marmont

Although built in the same period as the Hollywood Roosevelt Hotel, the Chateau Marmont has a tad more character. Nestled in the hills just above Sunset Boulevard, this landmark Hollywood hideaway was modeled after a French chateau. Fleur-de-lis patterns are carved into the gray stone walls, while Norman archways line a tranquil courtyard and croquet lawn. The wood-floored lobby has a clubby thirties atmosphere.

The adjacent cottages, on the other hand, are built in early California bungalow style. They're grouped in private niches around the swimming pool, where mostly youthful, hip-looking guests lounge about. Old Hollywood glamour might be alive and well at Chateau Marmont, but the clientele is definitely in the here and now.

CHATEAU MARMONT

Telephone: **(800) CHATEAU; (213) 656-1010; fax (213) 655-5311**
Address: **8221 Sunset Boulevard, Hollywood 90046**
Rates: **$170 to $1,200**
Directions: **on Sunset Boulevard, just west of Laurel Canyon Boulevard.**

LITTLE NOVELTY: The **Sunset Marquis Hotel and Villas** in West Hollywood has its own recording studio, complete with a video connection to the upstairs rock and roll pub. You can cut your own album here or watch the action from the pub. For more information, call (310) 657-1333.

LAKE ARROWHEAD

Bracken Fern Manor

Looking at it now, you'd never guess that Bracken Fern Manor was once owned by Bugsy Segal and run by the mob as a clubhouse for gambling and prostitution. This twenties Tudor-style inn has been so thoroughly remodeled that its neat-as-a-pin interior looks brand new. The only vestige left from its tarnished days is a trapdoor in the living room floor. It drops to a secret tunnel that leads under the street to another building where gambling once was a favorite pastime. Now that the days of Prohibition are long gone, periodic wine tastings are offered by the innkeepers in the cellar.

The immaculate guest rooms are all decorated in typical country inn style except for the Bridal Suite, which is all in white. Everything—from the sofa, to the gauzy netting surrounding the romantic canopy bed, to the bridal veil hanging on the mirror—is newlywed white. A playful touch in this room is the basket of bath toys at the Jacuzzi—not just the usual rubber ducky, mind you, but a whole basket filled with squirt guns, sailboats, and other nostalgic delights.

BRACKEN FERN MANOR

Telephone: **(909) 337-8557; fax (909) 337-3323**
Address: **815 Arrowhead Villas Road, P.O. Box 1006, Lake Arrowhead 92352**
Rates: **$75 to $175, including full breakfast**
Directions: **From SR-18 (quarter-mile after the SR-173 turn-off), turn left at Arrowhead Villas Road.**

LONG BEACH

The *Queen Mary*

Since it found a permanent berth in Long Beach Harbor in 1967, the *Queen Mary* has become an integral part of the city. Unbelievably, it was almost sold to Hong Kong for $20 million several years ago. Fortunately, the City of Long Beach changed its mind and has managed to hold onto it for another few years. It's one of the last remaining ships in the world that captures the glamour of thirties ocean liner travel. And best of all—you can spend the night aboard her.

First launched in 1934, the *Queen Mary* was the flagship of Britain's Cunard-White Star Line. Weighing 81,237 tons, her thousand-foot length was laid with fifty-six kinds of hardwood.

The vessel served variously as a luxury ocean liner and troop ship during World War II. Many of the rich and famous have crossed the Atlantic on this grand lady at one time or another—Winston Churchill, Fred Astaire, Bing Crosby, Rex Harrison, and Sir Alec Guinness, to name a few. Their photos are displayed throughout the ship.

Only in the sixties, when the airplane became a more effective means of transportation, was the *Queen Mary* put to rest in Long Beach. Now it's a hotel and shopping complex, with 365 staterooms and seventeen suites. Aside from six new restaurants (the original first-, second-, and third-class dining rooms are unused now) and historic displays throughout the ship, it remains largely unchanged from the first voyage sixty years ago. The decor—a mixture of art deco and industrial age—is divinely nostalgic, especially in the Observation Bar and the Grand Salon (the original first-class dining room). Curved sleekly into the bow, the Observation Bar is an atmospheric spot for a drink. It was used in a scene for the filming of *Barton Fink*.

Each stateroom is slightly different, but they all have richly paneled wood, art deco touches, and many original fixtures. Next to some of the bathtubs are buttons formerly used to summon male or female attendants to help passengers out of the tub in rough seas. Other rooms still have fold-out desks with built-in pipe and tobacco holders. When booking, be sure to ask for a starboard (right side) stateroom, which faces the harbor instead of the parking lot.

Two of the twelve decks are reserved exclusively for hotel guests, which is generous considering that more than a million people visit the *Queen Mary* every year. At night, when the tourists have gone home, you have the ship to yourself.

THE *QUEEN MARY*

Telephone: **(800) 437-2934; (310) 435-3511**
Address: **1126 Queens Highway, Long Beach 90802**
Rates: **$75 to $145**
Directions: **From I-710 south in Long Beach, follow signs to the *Queen Mary*.**

LOS ANGELES

The Westin Bonaventure

When the Bonaventure was built in 1976, it delivered a shot in the arm to downtown Los Angeles. Since then, the cityscape has never been the same. I lived nearby then and watched with anticipation as the massive cluster of reflective glass cylinders grew taller by the day. When the hotel opened, I went there with my college friends. Even then we were awestruck by the fantastic, futuristic atrium lobby. The glass elevators that shot up the outside of the building to the dizzying thirty-fifth floor were a real novelty then.

Years later I spent the night in a room on the thirtieth floor at bird's-eye level with the tops of the surrounding skyscrapers. Like all the rooms, one whole wall consisted of floor-to-ceiling glass with nothing beyond but a vertical drop. All night I kept dreaming my bed was sliding across the room and out the window.

Now called the Westin Bonaventure, this hotel might have lost some of its cutting-edge quality, but nonetheless, it's not for the faint of heart. That elevator ride is still unnerving.

THE WESTIN BONAVENTURE

Telephone: **(800) 228-3000; (213) 624-1000; fax (213) 612-4894**
Address: **404 South Figueroa Street, Los Angeles 90071**
Rates: **$109 to $195**
Directions: **From I-110 north, exit at Third Street and turn right, then right on Flower Street. From I-110 south, exit at Wilshire Boulevard and turn left, then left on Figueroa Street and right on Fourth Street.**

The Biltmore Los Angeles

Built by the same architects who designed the Waldorf-Astoria, the Biltmore Los Angeles rivals the grandest hotels in Europe. The public rooms—especially the ornate ceilings—are visually stunning. Among the most extraordinary rooms are the main lobby, the Rendezvous Court, the indoor swimming pool, and the Crystal Ballroom (where the founding banquet for the Academy of Motion Picture Arts and Sciences was held). The Crystal Ballroom's ceiling was hand painted by Italian artist Giovanni Smeraldi.

Since it opened in 1923, the Biltmore has hosted countless dignitaries and served as the backdrop for many films (*Chinatown, The Sting,* and *A Star is Born,* to name a few). For two thousand dollars you can sleep in the three-bedroom Presidential Suite where Truman, Kennedy, Ford, Carter, Reagan, and Clinton have stayed.

THE BILTMORE LOS ANGELES

Telephone: **(800) 245-8673; (213) 612-1575; fax (213) 612-1545**
Address: **506 South Grand Avenue, Los Angeles 90071**
Rates: **$195 to $2,000**
Directions: **in downtown Los Angeles, between Fifth and Sixth Streets.**

The New Otani Hotel & Garden

East meets west at the New Otani Hotel & Garden in downtown Los Angeles, where you can spend the night in one of three traditional Japanese suites. Each suite overlooks the hotel's Japanese garden and features a sitting room of tatami mats and shoji screens (with Japanese slippers awaiting at the entry), a bedroom with platform bed, and a Japanese sunken tub in the bathroom. If you want to go the gamut, book their "Japanese Experience" package: a night in a Japanese suite, a welcome cup of sake, dinner for two at their Japanese restaurant, a shiatsu massage, sauna, Jacuzzi, and a western or Japanese champagne breakfast in the morning. Oh, and you get to take home a live bonsai tree. *Yokoso*—enter and enjoy.

THE NEW OTANI HOTEL & GARDEN

Telephone: **(800) 273-2294; (213) 629-1200; fax (213) 622-0980**
Address: **120 South Los Angeles Street, Los Angeles 90012**
Rates: **$155 to $1,500, single; $180 to $1,500, double; $599 for Japanese Experience package**
Directions: **on Los Angeles Street, between First and Second Streets.**

Hotel Bel-Air

After a long, hot day of battling traffic, I pulled off Sunset Boulevard and drove up Stone Canyon through a cool tunnel of trees to the Hotel Bel-Air. The mere sight of it was soothing to my rattled senses. Instead of a flashy, sterilized hotel that blared out its status, here was an oasis of low-key, Old California charm. Buffered by twelve acres of verdant gardens, the informal reception building has uncarpeted wood floors and the comforting smell of real wood burning in the fireplace. The pink Mediterranean-style villas are hidden away among the trees, with vines of greenery and bougainvillea trailing untamed over red tiled roofs.

Although no measure of comfort has been spared here, the grounds are what make the Bel-Air so utterly romantic. Little foot bridges span back and forth over a rambling creek and waterfalls, while white swans rest on the banks. Huge sycamores, redwoods, and tree ferns filter out the sunlight, keeping the air cool and moist. The sweet fragrances and singing birds are a rarity so close to the concrete-covered city. Here, all is unhurried.

It's understandable why celebrities and dignitaries have been escaping to the Hotel Bel-Air for more than fifty years. It's more like a private enchanted estate than a hotel.

HOTEL BEL-AIR

Telephone:	**(800) 648-4097; (310) 472-1211; fax (310) 476-5890**
Address:	**701 Stone Canyon Road, Los Angeles 90077**
Rates:	**$285 to $2,500**
Directions:	**on Stone Canyon Road, off Sunset Boulevard, above UCLA.**

NEWPORT BEACH

Worldwide Boat & Breakfast

"Boat and breakfasts" are a growing trend and playful twist to the traditional bed and breakfast concept—an overnight on a private luxury yacht with breakfast delivered to your cabin door. Sometimes charter trips can be arranged, but usually the vessels remain moored in the harbor.

Worldwide Boat & Breakfast in Newport Harbor is one of two boat and breakfast enterprises that have sprouted up along the California coast. The luxury power and sailing yachts, ranging in length from thirty-five to eighty-two feet, are docked at various spots around the harbor. Although they differ in amenities, all come equipped with televisions, VCRs, fresh flowers, galleys, and maid service. One yacht even has a Jacuzzi in its master stateroom. The *Bounty* is the most unique of them all. Built in 1934, this restored seventy-two-foot ketch is quite romantic: a dozen people have proposed marriage on it. Its polished teak interior, stained glass, and rose velvet decor create a warm environment. The satin sheets and candles don't hurt, either.

But the best part of this overnight attraction is owner and "boatkeeper" Vili Boyadjiev, an attractive woman who packs an incredible amount of energy into her petite frame. Born and raised in Bulgaria, Vili worked there as a professional singer until she fled the country in the mid-1980s. She looks wonderfully incongruous clacking around the boat docks in her high heels, dressed to the nines, chatting away with her exotic accent. She has trained her mascot parrot, Julio, to greet people at the office with "Book a boat! Book a boat!"

All of Vili's yachts are available for "Snooze and Cruise" excursions around the harbor. She also offers a "Yachts of Bubbles" ride, where up to six people can cruise around the harbor soaking in a deck-top Jacuzzi.

WORLDWIDE BOAT & BREAKFAST

Telephone: **(800) BOAT-BED; (714) 723-5552; fax (714) 723-4626**
Address: **3400 Via Oporto, Suite 103, Newport Beach 92663**
Rates: **$150 to $400, including continental breakfast**
Directions: **From Pacific Coast Highway, exit at Newport Boulevard and head down the peninsula; turn left at the Lido Theatre and look for the Worldwide Boat & Breakfast office at the Via Oporto intersection.**

Doryman's Inn Bed & Breakfast

Doryman's Inn is a luxurious surprise considering its understated exterior and low-key location across from the Newport Pier fish market. Even the entrance offers no hint of the opulence that lies within—only an unmarked elevator. You don't get the full effect until you reach the second floor.

The first time those elevator doors opened for me, I was astonished at the sumptuous scene. Classical music drifted down the fern-filled, skylit hallway to one exquisite bedroom after another. Every room has lush carpets and drapes, carved or canopied beds, gas fireplaces with beautifully carved mantels, and Italian marble sunken tubs. On top of all that, they are furnished with a host of luxuries not often found at a bed and breakfast—delicate glass mantelpiece clocks, old-fashioned telephones, beveled mirrors behind the beds, and gilt-edged nineteenth-century paintings (mostly of loosely clad women). Rooms Six and Eight are particularly stunning with their lavishly draped canopy beds.

DORYMAN'S INN BED & BREAKFAST

Telephone: (714) 675-7300
Address: 2102 West Ocean Front, Newport Beach 92663
Rates: $135 to $275, including breakfast
Directions: From the Coast Highway, take Balboa Boulevard to MacFadden Place and turn right; follow the signs to the Newport Pier, which is opposite the inn.

PASADENA

The Ritz-Carlton Huntington Hotel

Even though most of it was torn down and rebuilt in 1990, the Ritz-Carlton Huntington Hotel perseveres as a major landmark in Pasadena. One thing that makes the hotel particularly distinctive is its unique Picture Bridge. The redwood footbridge was built in 1914 to span an arroyo to the hotel's cottages. Murals were added in the thirties after a guest remarked that the covered bridge reminded her of a similar bridge in Lucerne. In exchange for ten dollars per painting and all the food he could eat, British landscape artist Frank Montague Moore painted forty-one scenes of California landmarks—everything from Death Valley to the Huntington Library—across the triangular gables of the bridge. Poet Donald Blanding composed the accompanying verses attached to the posts.

THE RITZ-CARLTON HUNTINGTON HOTEL

Telephone: (800) 241-3333; (818) 568-3900; fax (818) 568-3700
Address: 1401 South Oak Knoll Avenue, Pasadena 91106
Rates: $165 to $1,500
Directions: When I-110 north ends in Pasadena, turn right at Glenarm Street (the first stoplight), right on El Molino Street, left on Eliott Street, and right on Oak Knoll Avenue.

REDLANDS

Morey Mansion Bed & Breakfast Inn

One of the most architecturally eclectic buildings you'll ever see, Morey Mansion is crowned by its Russian "onion" dome, French Mansard roof, and Chinese verandah. David Morey, a retired ship-builder/cabinetmaker, handcrafted in 1890 this one-of-a-kind, twenty-room mansion for his beloved wife out of bits and pieces of architecture he had seen during his travels around the world. The oak interior is rich with his elaborate woodwork designs of flowers, fish, fruit, anchors, and dragon tails. The reception hall is carved to depict the inside of a ship's captain's quarters. The four pillars that support the library archway are all carved differently. Throughout the entire mansion, no two carvings are exactly alike.

Morey Mansion's architecture represents bits and pieces from around the world.

MOREY MANSION BED & BREAKFAST INN

Telephone: **(909) 793-7970; fax (909) 793-7870**
Address: **190 Terracina Boulevard, Redlands 92373**
Rates: **$109 to $145, including continental breakfast**
Directions: **From I-10, exit at Alabama Avenue in Redlands and head south; after two miles, turn right on Barton Road, then left on Terracina Boulevard. Tours every Sunday from 12 noon to 3 P.M.**

The Mission Inn occupies an entire city block in downtown Riverside.

RIVERSIDE

Mission Inn

Covering an entire city block of downtown Riverside, the Mission Inn is a veritable maze of turrets and domes, spiraling staircases and arcades, catacombs, and carillon towers. Its ornate architecture and elaborate display of stained glass, wrought iron, ceramic tiles, saints, dragons, and bells are an extraordinary feast for the eyes—a fantastic cross between a California mission and a Moorish castle.

The Mission Inn began as a small adobe boardinghouse in 1876 and expanded to its present size over the course of fifty-five years. After eccentric owner-designer Frank Miller died in the 1930s, the landmark hotel went through a litany of owners but never lacked famous guests. Roosevelt, Taft, Reagan, and Bogart all stayed here. Pat and Richard Nixon were married here in 1940. But gradually the hotel fell into decline. In 1985, it closed for a two-year renovation, but didn't reopen until seven years later. It was closed for so long, in fact, that everyone wondered, "What ever happened to the Mission Inn?"

Upon visiting the newly renovated Mission Inn, I was relieved to find it well worth the wait. Every detail has been magnificently restored, from the top of its chiming bell towers to its tiled courtyards. The central Spanish Courtyard, best viewed from the fourth floor, is marvelously embellished with Moorish archways and turrets, elaborate grillwork, and gargoyles. There is even a statue of a big bear among the mission figures on the rooftops—all symbolic of early California.

Across a narrow outdoor bridge on the fourth floor is the Rotunda Wing, where there is a five-story spiral staircase, an exquisite chapel, art gallery, and Fliers Wall—a monument to pioneers in aviation. The St. Francis Chapel, built to accommodate a massive gold-leafed cedar altar from Mexico, features seven Tiffany stained-glass windows.

Every guest room has a different configuration, and many still have low arched entries. My favorite rooms are the two-level suites with balconies along Author's Row, again on the fourth level.

The kaleidoscope-like details go on and on, but you really need to see it yourself. This is not a place that can be absorbed quickly. If you are visiting the hotel for the first time, consider taking a tour. Tours begin every half hour on Saturdays and Sundays and four times on weekdays.

MISSION INN

Telephone: **(800) 843-7755; (909) 784-0300**
Address: **3649 Seventh Street, Riverside 92501**
Rates: **$145 to $530**
Directions: **From SR-91 south, exit at Seventh Street and head west three blocks. From SR-91 north, exit at University Avenue, drive one block north to Seventh Street, and head west.**

3 CENTRAL COAST

Crystal Rose Inn

This three-story Victorian structure makes quite a sight, towering out of the flat farmlands in multiple shades of pink. Reminiscent of a peppermint ice-cream cone, the Crystal Rose Inn (formerly the Rose Victorian Inn) is steeped in old-fashioned romance.

Bathed in various shades of pink, Crystal Rose Inn resembles a peppermint ice-cream cone.

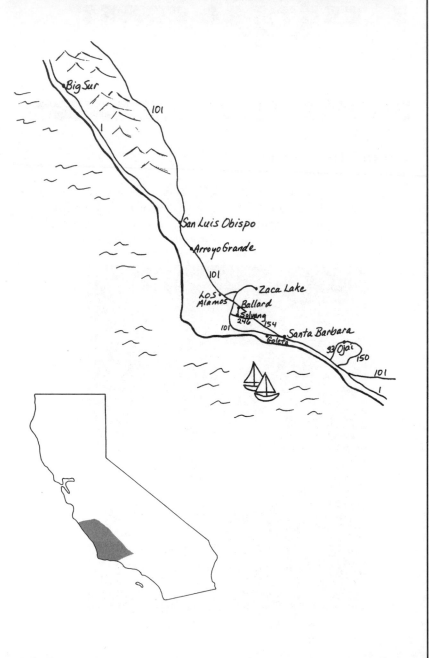

Among the guest rooms (each named after a favorite rose of the innkeeper), the Queen Elizabeth Tower Suite is most unusual. A little door leads from the bathroom up narrow stairs to a secret hideaway in the tower. Another pretty room is the Honor Suite, decorated all in white—an obvious choice for honeymooners.

Wandering around the impeccable lawns and rose gardens, it's easy to see why weddings are a big deal here—big enough to have an on-site wedding coordinator. To date, more than six hundred couples have been married in the gazebo, and under the shade of the inn's old ash tree.

Crystal Rose Inn also has a restaurant. High tea is served every afternoon, both to the public and guests. The numerous packages offered include art, gardening, and cooking classes.

CRYSTAL ROSE INN

Telephone:	**(800) ROSE-INN; (805) 481-1854; fax (805) 481-9541**
Address:	**789 Valley Road, Arroyo Grande 93420**
Rates:	**$85 to $175, including full breakfast, high tea, and evening hors d'oeuvres**
Directions:	**From US-101, exit at Fair Oaks Avenue and head west; turn left on Valley Road.**

BALLARD

The Ballard Inn

Of the Victorian, vineyard, and western-inspired guest rooms at the Ballard Inn, the Old West themes are the most playful. The Western Room, for instance, features chaps and a cow skull hanging on the wall, and a log cabin patchwork quilt on the bed. Davy Brown's Room (named after a famous mountain man of the area) has the feel of a log cabin, with weathered wood paneling and floors, a stone fireplace, rockers, and various rustic touches—a long rifle here and a whiskey jug there.

It's easy to imagine the days of the early cattle ranchers and frontiersmen in a town such as Ballard—the oldest town in the Santa Ynez Valley—because it's still so small and sleepy. But the Ballard Inn is about as civilized as a country inn can get. There are wineries galore in this area, and in the afternoons you can sample local libations with hors d'oeuvres in a tasting room at the inn. The inn also has a full-service restaurant, the Café Chardonnay. I especially liked the Stagecoach Lounge. To reach the restrooms, you pass through saloon-style swinging doors.

THE BALLARD INN

Telephone: **(800) 638-2466; (805) 688-7770; fax (805) 688-9560**
Address: **2436 Baseline Avenue, Ballard 93463**
Rates: **$160 to $195, including full breakfast and afternoon wine and hors d'oeuvres**
Directions: **From SR-154 in Los Olivos or Route 246 in Solvang, take Alamo Pintado Road to Ballard, and turn right on Baseline Road.**

BIG SUR

Esalen Institute

Ask anyone in the "New Age-know" about Esalen. Watch their eyes glaze over and their mouths turn up in an enigmatic smile. This is where such activities as gestalt, rolfing, and Feldenkrais first got started in California. For more than thirty years, this Big Sur retreat has been offering seminars, workshops, and residential work-study programs centered around what they call Experimental Education. Among the wildly varying workshops scheduled about two times a week are "Vision Painting," "Massage Mbunde," "the Singing Cure," "Brain Wave Training," "Jewish Humor," "Chi Gung," "When Drummers Were Women," and even one called "the Ultimate Yes."

I can't resist a few jabs at the spirithead mentality that pervades Esalen, but—all kidding aside—I would love to stay here someday. Its dramatic cliffside location high above the ocean is spectacular; the hot mineral spring tubs and outdoor massage areas (both clothing-optional) are in an open-air building that literally hangs from the side of a cliff above the ocean; and out of the five hundred workshops a year, there is something for everyone— yoga, art, wilderness programs—you name it. If you're coming for the first time and are not sure what to take, try the "experiencing Esalen" workshop, which offers an introduction to gestalt, massage, sensory awareness, and meditation.

Although workshops are top priority at Esalen, you don't have to participate to stay here. If they have extra space after the workshops are booked and you call fewer than five days ahead, they'll accept shorter, less involved stays. Some activities such as the morning movement classes, baths, and massages are always available to overnighters. But generally, very few people stay at Esalen for just one night. This is a place where it takes time to immerse oneself. Some wind up working here for a month while they take classes—a great way to reduce expenses. They offer senior citizens' discounts, too.

The accommodations vary widely, from the old quarters of early convicts (who once worked on Highway One), to fifties-style buildings, to a nice Victorian house. There are also dorm bunk beds and sleeping bag spaces. You can't request a particular building—where you are placed depends on where your seminar is scheduled. But couples will always be housed together, and childcare is provided for families.

Elsewhere on the rambling grounds are a swimming pool (clothing-optional), organic garden, meditation house, art center, and cafeteria. Check out the staff's living quarters, hugging a cliff-side ravine over the ocean—they have the best seats in the house!

ESALEN INSTITUTE

Telephone: **(408) 667-3000 for first-timers; (408) 644-8477 for repeat guests who know what they want; (408) 644-8476 for catalog requests**
Address: **Highway 1, Big Sur 93920.**
Rates: **$70 to $125 per person, including dinner, breakfast and lunch; weekend, five-day, and seven-day rates also available; additional cost for workshops**
Directions: **on Highway 1, fifty miles north of San Simeon, eleven miles south of Big Sur; no drop-ins or visitors—open by reservation only.**

Deetjen's Big Sur Inn

When Helmuth and Helen Deetjen moved to Big Sur from Norway in the early thirties, Highway 1 was little more than a wagon road. The Deetjens began welcoming overnight guests who stopped to rest on their way up and down the long, winding coastal route. Eventually, they added guest rooms and rustic cabins, building them out of scavenged redwood in the style of their native Norway. When "Grandpa" Deetjen died in 1972, he left the inn to "transient guests so that the public may enjoy the natural beauty, charm, and scenery of the Big Sur Inn." As a result, Deetjen's Big Sur Inn is now operated on a nonprofit basis by a preservation foundation.

Nestled snugly in a lush canyon, the cabins are situated above a babbling brook that you can hear from your bed (one advantage of the paper-thin walls). They have a wonderful, rustic charm, with dark wood floors and walls, hooked rugs, handhewn Dutch doors, no locks (although the doors can be secured from within), and many fireplaces or wood-burning stoves. The little adjacent restaurant, which was Grandpa Deetjen's original house, is warm and informal.

DEETJEN'S BIG SUR INN

Telephone: **(408) 667-2377**
Address: **Highway 1, Big Sur 93920**
Rates: **$70 to $150**
Directions: **on Highway 1, three miles south of Pfeiffer Big Sur State Park.**

Post Ranch Inn

Architecturally, the Post Ranch Inn is one of the most environmentally sensitive lodgings in this state. Perched high on a ridge above the Big Sur coastline, all thirty guest units are designed to have a minimal impact on the surrounding landscape. Some sit on stilts among the redwoods (in order to protect the tree roots); others are recessed into the side of the ridge with sod roofs. There are also cylinder-shaped units and a three-level, angular "Butterfly House." For the entire hundred-acre project, only one single tree was removed.

According to architect Mickey Muennig, each structure is supposed to relate to the environment so that people will feel a part of nature, not merely observers of it. It worked for me. When I walked into their glass-enclosed restaurant, which clings

Guest units at the Post Ranch Inn come in many shapes and sizes.

impossibly close to the edge of the ridge, I suddenly felt detached from the cliff, suspended in the sky.

The construction of the guest units is intentionally spare, airy, and Zenlike, with natural wood, slate floors, lots of glass, and skylights. The comforters on the platform beds are made from recycled denim; the hardwoods are unendangered; guests can sort out their glass, paper, and plastic in bins provided. Earth-friendly as they might be, the guests units aren't without their luxuries—fireplaces, minibars, state-of-the-art music systems, spas, and massage tables for guests who want a stay-at-home massage. The sense of peace is enhanced by the lack of cars—guests park down the hill and shuttle back and forth.

All of this novelty doesn't come cheaply. A night in a tree house, for instance, is around four hundred dollars; a sod-roofed ocean house—five hundred dollars. Yes, they are environmentally correct; economically, perhaps another story.

POST RANCH INN

Telephone: **(800) 527-2200; (408) 667-2200; fax (408) 667-2824**
Address: **Highway 1, P.O. Box 219, Big Sur 93920**
Rates: **$265 to $900, including continental breakfast**
Directions: **on Highway 1, two and one-half miles south of Pfeiffer Big Sur State Park**
(across from Ventana Inn).

GOLETA

Circle Bar B Guest Ranch

Circle Bar B Guest Ranch probably comes closer to one's idea of a classic dude ranch than any other lodging in Southern California. Run by the Brown family since the late thirties, the ranch is now enjoying its third generation of owners. Located in the foothills above Goleta (just down the road from Reagan's ranch), Circle Bar B encompasses nearly a thousand acres of countryside. All of the traditional guest ranch offerings are provided—trail rides, horseback riding lessons for all levels, weekend poolside barbecues, hiking, and even dinner theater productions in the old barn. The all-inclusive informal meals are served at long picnic tables.

Accommodations, ranging from a room in the ranch house to a private cabin with wood-burning fireplace, are more upscale than one might expect. Crisp and new-looking, they're accented by clever western touches. For instance, you might find the wingback chairs covered in cowhide print, or the shower curtains tied back with red bandannas, or the beds built of bent willow.

Altogether, Circle Bar B is a super place for families. Children under three stay free, and older children cost only $60 extra per day, with all meals included. The cabins also have sleeping lofts for children.

CIRCLE BAR B GUEST RANCH

Telephone: **(805) 968-1113**
Address: **1800 Refugio Road, Goleta 93117**
Rates: **$186 to $225, including all meals**
Directions: **From US-101 north of Goleta, exit at Refugio Road and head inland.**

LOS ALAMOS

The Victorian Mansion and Union Hotel

The Victorian Mansion wins my vote as the most offbeat overnight in California. If you're looking for a thoroughly novel experience, it doesn't get any better than this.

Have your next toga party in the Victorian Mansion's Roman Room.

Situated in a tiny village north of Solvang, the three-story Victorian Mansion looks deceptively normal on the outside. But hidden behind its facade are a collection of six theme rooms embellished to the hilt. Take my room, for example—the Fifties Drive-In Room. The bed is an authentic Cadillac convertible parked before a movie screen just as if it were at the drive-in. The rear fender and taillights are converted into a coffee table, and the detached trunk is built into a sink. Walls are decorated with colorful neon lights and hand-painted murals depicting a whimsical fifties drive-in scene, complete with a night sky and stars on the ceiling. Hidden behind a secret door, the bathroom is covered in "Kilroy was here" graffiti. The cassette player comes equipped with fifties music, the video selections are from the fifties, and a Monopoly game completes the picture. We watched *Rebel Without a Cause* (with the sound coming from a drive-in speaker) through the windshield of the Caddy in our surprisingly comfortable car bed.

The Egyptian Room, accessed by a heavy stone door, is swathed like a harem, with canopied bed and ceilings, and Oriental rugs. To get into the bathroom, which is guarded by King Tut himself, you pull on his beard. The accompanying music is Middle Eastern.

Enjoy the backseat in the Fifties Drive-in Room at the Victorian Mansion.

If it's ancient Rome you're yearning for, you can sleep in a silver chariot in the Roman Room. Marble steps lead up to the soaking tub. Roman columns, busts, and trompe l'oeil murals of burning Rome surround the room. Your video selection is, what else, but *Ben Hur.*

In the Pirate Room, you're inside a swashbucklers' pirate ship with wood paneling, stained glass, and dramatically pitched, asymmetrical ceilings. The coffee table is perched atop a cannon, while an open treasure chest sits by the cabin-style bed. Footprints on the bathroom floor lead to a surprise in the shower. The background music consists of thunderstorms at sea, and one of the movie selections is *Captain Blood.*

You can also sleep in a gypsy wagon and read tarot cards to each other in the Gypsy Room, amid forest sounds of frogs and babbling brooks. Or, if you want a slightly more subdued fantasy, try the Parisian Room, with its fainting couch and loft bed accessed by an iron spiral stairway. The mural in the elegant little bathroom is quite clever—scenes from the Paris opera and *Follies Bergère* surround you, and the floor tiles are painted to give the appearance of roses cast at your feet.

Each room comes equipped with a television, VCR, fireplace, soaking tub, minirefrigerator with complimentary champagne, and cassette player. Everything, including the lights, is turned on and off via remote control. Even though the innkeeper spends an introductory ten minutes explaining the intricacies of this remote, it takes the concentration of a rocket scientist to figure it out. You'll probably spend the first half-hour, as we did, just switching everything on and off. Even the bath water is turned on by remote and automatically stops when it reaches a certain level. It's all a bit unnerving (especially when everything is on at once), but it adds to the fun.

In the morning, breakfast is delivered by a dumbwaiter concealed behind yet another secret door. A buzzer goes off at 8:30 and suddenly there is your coffee and juice. At nine o'clock, another buzzer, and *voilà,* it's the rest of your breakfast.

Next to the Victorian Mansion is an Old West-style building called the Union Hotel, part of the same operation. On the outside it looks intriguing—the front is covered with wooden planks from various barns and sheds. But the small upstairs guest rooms, with their modest country Victorian decor, don't hold a candle to the Victorian Mansion. The building does, however, contain a wonderful saloon, a restaurant where guests can have dinner, and a billiards room. Also on the grounds are a swimming pool, gazebo hot tub, and old-fashioned garden maze.

This amazing fantasy was created by Dick Langdon, an obvious eccentric who passed away several years ago. It took nine years and two hundred craftsmen to complete the whole project. If you have a few minutes, check out the before-and-after photos in the lobby album. The transformation is simply incredible. Why he picked such a diminutive town to build in is anyone's guess. But the Victorian Mansion is a destination inn anyway—once you check in, you won't want to leave the property. It's a great place to bring someone for a special occasion—someone with a sense of humor, that is. My personal romantic favorite is the Egyptian Room, but even the Fifties Room—despite its cramped bathroom and Mickey Mouse comforter on the bed—is playfully romantic. The hardest choice is deciding which room to stay in. But be sure to call ahead; the inn books up several months in advance. Also, ask them to send you a brochure—it's as big as a restaurant menu.

THE VICTORIAN MANSION AND UNION HOTEL

Telephone: **(800) 230-2744; (805) 344-2744; fax (805) 344-3125**
Address: **362 Bell Street, P.O. Box 616, Los Alamos 93440**
Rates: **$200, including breakfast, in the Victorian Mansion; $80 to $100, including breakfast, in the Union Hotel. Union Hotel open weekends only.**
Directions: **From US-101, exit at Los Alamos and head down the main street—you can't miss it.**

OJAI

Ojai Valley Inn

Since the Ojai Valley Inn was remodeled, a new reception building and conference center have been added, giving the old country club a split personality. These new buildings do not have a lot of character; unfortunately, they are what you first encounter when you drive up. But take the time to walk past these institutional structures, through the beautifully landscaped grounds, and back to the old section. You'll find a completely different Ojai Valley Inn. Terraced down the hillside and overlooking the hotel's beautiful golf course are the original twenties clubhouse cottages. The historic Hacienda has been restored to the original California Mission style of the twenties and thirties. Its guest rooms feature century-old hardwood floors, mission-period wrought-iron sconces, and hand-painted tiles.

Although the resort offers the usual activities such as tennis, horseback riding, and swimming pools, most people come here for the exquisite golf course. Its undulating hills, old trestle bridges, and oak trees look positively ethereal at times. The stunning Topa Topa Mountains are visible in all directions. The golf course was designed by Billy Bell in the twenties and updated by Jay Morrish in the eighties. A round of golf doesn't come cheaply, but the inn does offer slightly discounted golf packages for guests.

OJAI VALLEY INN

Telephone:	**(800) 422-OJAI; (805) 646-5511; fax (805) 646-7969**
Address:	**Country Club Road, Ojai 93023**
Rates:	**$195 to $850**
Directions:	**From SR-150 east in Ojai, turn right on Country Club Road.**

The Ojai Foundation

The Ojai Foundation is self-described as a "land-based educational sanctuary for youth and adults." "Land-based" means it's very rustic. Situated on a forty-acre plateau of semiwilderness in the upper Ojai Valley, the dwellings (called "hermitages") consist of tepees, yurts, domes, and campsites connected by a meandering stone path. Hot showers and community restrooms are provided, but you must bring your own food and bedding. Individuals can stay from one to thirty days and are invited to participate in daily meditation and weekly councils. Solitary time is also encouraged. A retreat coordinator is available to help design your "time on the land."

The Ojai Foundation is a back-to-the-land sort of place. Although the foundation offers both private and public seminars on a wide variety of subjects—from the Mystery of Eros in Relationships to Transformative Council for Mature Women—it's primarily a place to heal and commune with nature. It's ideally poised above the Ojai Valley (the site of Shangri-La in the film *Paradise Lost*) within a circle of craggy mountains. The scent of native plants—lavender, sage, and, unfortunately, poison oak—is pungent here. The drive to the site is through a field of sunflowers. While wandering the grounds, I passed a woman toiling in the garden (some participants here are on work exchange). What a nice retreat this would be for one going through a difficult stage in need of some earthy healing time. Indeed, the main focus of the workshops seems to be on rites of passage, for all ages.

The map at the entrance points out the earth shrine, sky dancing ground, oak medicine tepee, sweat lodge, pottery studio, and medicine wheel. Ceremonies are big here.

THE OJAI FOUNDATION

Telephone: **(805) 646-8343**
Address: **P.O. Box 1620, Ojai 93024**
Rates: **$30 to $40 per person**
Directions: **east of Ojai on SR-150.**

SAN LUIS OBISPO

Sycamore Mineral Springs Resort

If you like hot tubs, you've got plenty of 'em at Sycamore Mineral Springs Resort. Not only are there twenty redwood hot tubs nestled on the hillside, but each guest room has a hot tub on its own private balcony. And if that's not enough, the resort has a big group spa that holds up to forty people.

These naturally hot, sulfur-based mineral springs have been drawing visitors since the turn of the century (W. C. Fields was a frequent guest). In the 1930s, when it was a therapeutic center, people came for mineral water treatments to cure aches and pains. Today, this small, quiet resort offers motel-type guest rooms and suites terraced steeply up the hillside, as well as a restaurant, swimming pool, and spa building where massages are offered. You don't have to stay here to have a massage or use the hillside tubs (which actually have more ambiance than do the guest room tubs). With names such as Xanadu, Atlantis, and Erehwon, the hillside tubs are comfortably spaced among the oak and sycamore trees, affording plenty of privacy. The wooded setting and soothing sound of wind chimes make me want to come here just for a massage-and-hot-tub combo.

SYCAMORE MINERAL SPRINGS RESORT

Telephone: **(800) 234-5831; (805) 595-7302**
Address: **1215 Avila Beach Drive, San Luis Obispo 93405**
Rates: **$104 to $145**
Directions: **From US-101 south of San Luis Obispo, exit at Sycamore Mineral Springs.**

Madonna Inn

The Madonna Inn is probably better known than any other hotel in the world for its fantasy rooms. This swirling, pink confection has riveted the attention of Highway 101 travelers since the late fifties. Tourists stop here just to gape, laugh, and try out the restrooms, which are a kick. The hotel is incredibly gaudy and so wildly popular that its one hundred-plus theme rooms are booked year-round.

From the outside, the main building and guest quarters look like the tiers of an elaborate wedding cake, with pink and white trim and filigree everywhere. To describe the interior as excessively ornate is an understatement. At the entrance to the restaurant, a massive tangle of artificial vines, flowers, tiny white lights, and cherubs weave above the circular, hot-pink leather dining booths. Rising out of the center of the room is a huge, gold candelabra-like tree crafted from leftover electrical conduit, scrap copper, and spare diesel fuel tubing.

Moving next door to the coffee shop, I couldn't find one square inch of plain surface. (A wood carver spent ten years on the wood alone.) The circular counter and red leather stools are

The Madonna Inn's Caveman Room even includes a rock waterfall shower.

reminiscent of a carousel ride. Pink cakes piled ridiculously high with icing and big pink chunks occupy the display case in the adjoining bakery. The room is thick with the smell of sugar and butter.

The women's room includes a miniature sink and toilet just for little girls. But the biggest attraction is the wine cellar men's room. (In fact, so many women are constantly peeking in, I'm amazed that men get any privacy.) The urinal, which is built of rock, is designed so that when you stand before it, an electronic sensor triggers a waterfall down the rocks in front of you. No kidding. A postcard of the urinal is for sale.

Alex and Phyllis Madonna, the owners and decorators, make it abundantly clear they are partial to pink. (They decided it was a flattering color to women.) They offer pink ice buckets, pink sugar, waiters with pink bow ties, pink guest rooms (the Sugar 'n Spice Room is particularly intense), and even pink paper bags for gift shop purchases. Not just any pink, mind you, but

Madonna pink—a strong bubble-gum color reminiscent of Barbie Doll outfits from the sixties.

As for the guest rooms, where to begin? Every room is a different shape, and the themes range from primal rock rooms (the most fun) to the ethereal blue Just Heaven, with its spiral staircase ascending into a turret. Some, like the Madonna and Travelers' Suites, have humongous rock fireplaces. You can pick a room where the furnishings are the focal point (such as the barrel-filled Barrel of Fun), or where a particular country is the theme (such as the Matterhorn Room or Austrian Suite).

The themes are carried through to all of the bathrooms, too. In Cabin Still, for instance, the bathroom is built like an old-fashioned still. The Caveman Room, booked solid a year in advance, has rock walls, floors, and ceilings, and a rock waterfall shower.

All rooms look like they're stuck in a sixties time warp. It's not that they're worn, because the carpets and furnishings (which, my tour director earnestly pointed out, are only the finest) are replaced regularly. But the style never, ever changes. Some of the rooms still have daisy wallpaper, sparkly ceilings, and Naugahyde couches. And they have a loyal following. Some Madonna Inn guests request the same room every year and would be upset if anything changed.

This place is a landmark in Central California. It's like Disneyland on acid. In no other country could a hotel get away with being this deliciously garish—only in America, God bless her.

MADONNA INN

Telephone: **(800) 543-9666; (805) 543-3000; fax (805 543-1800**
Address: **100 Madonna Road, San Luis Obispo 93405**
Rates: **$77 to $210**
Directions: **From US-101, exit at Madonna Road.**

Garden Street Inn

Baseball fans will enjoy the Field of Dreams Room at the Garden Street Inn. Named in honor of owner Kathy Smith's father, who was a veteran sportswriter, the mostly green Field of Dreams guest room is decorated with baseball pennants, vintage baseball dolls with bobbing heads, and photos of famous players. A collection of marbles tops off the boyish nostalgia. This is a good room to book if you're bringing a jockish sort of guy to a bed and breakfast for the first time.

Set within walking distance of downtown San Luis Obispo and one block from the mission, this neat-as-a-pin Victorian inn features other theme rooms that are more subdued or in some cases completely obscure. Amadeus, which consists of a few music posters, is a nod to the local summer Mozart festival. Ah Louis, with its exotic bed, is a reminder of the town's Chinese heritage. There's also a tribute to *Our Town* and butterflies, among other eclectic motifs.

GARDEN STREET INN

Telephone: **(805) 545-9802**
Address: **1212 Garden Street, San Luis Obispo 93401**
Rates: **$90 to $160, including full breakfast**
Directions: **From US-101, exit at Marsh Street and turn right on Garden Street.**

Apple Farm Inn

The Apple Farm Inn is neither a farm nor an out-in-the-country inn as its name might suggest. Located on one of the main drags in San Luis Obispo, it's a large, busy, attractive inn with all the amenities of an upscale hotel. The property, which includes sixty-nine Victorian country rooms (all with fireplaces), two gift shops, a restaurant, swimming pool, and working mill house, is as clean as a whistle. The staff looks like they were recruited straight from Disneyland—friendly, clean-cut, and uniformed, right down to their walkie-talkies.

True to its name, the apple theme is everywhere. Each guest room has a red wooden apple you can take home with you. Your welcome basket includes chocolates, nuts, and sparkling apple cider. The gift shops display apples everywhere.

The main novelty here is the circa 1871 gristmill, which grinds wheat, churns ice cream, and presses (what else?) apple cider. Visitors can watch the fourteen-foot waterwheel at work and wander around inside the mill. There are two suites built into the upper floor of the mill house. Millhouse Suite B has a

The Apple Farm Inn's main novelty is the gristmill, circa 1871.

masculine decor, whereas Suite A is lighter and more feminine. The inn has two octagonal rooms in the main building; one is situated beneath the lobby and is somewhat noisy.

In the evenings, horse-drawn carriages pull up to the entry for those who wish to take a jaunt around town. The rides range from thirty minutes in the local neighborhood to sixty minutes all the way through town to the San Luis Obispo Mission.

APPLE FARM INN

Telephone: **(800) 374-3705**
Address: **2015 Monterey, San Luis Obispo 93401**
Rates: **$80 to $225; continental breakfast included in Trellis Court rooms**
Directions: **From US-101, exit at Monterey Street.**

SANTA BARBARA

Simpson House Inn

While Santa Barbara is full of lovely bed and breakfasts, the Simpson House Inn is my first choice. This stately Eastlake mansion is hidden behind a high hedge; one could easily drive right by without even noticing it. But inside the grounds—from the English gardens to the elegant interiors—everything is simply exquisite. The fabrics, wall coverings, Oriental rugs, and period beds are of the finest quality. The afternoon hors d'oeuvres and local wines are above the norm. And the gourmet morning repast, which begins with juice freshly squeezed from organically grown fruit, is superb.

Although the bedrooms in the main house are grand enough, I'm partial to the less formal garden cottages and the restored 1878 barn behind the house. Nestled invitingly under the trees, the cottages have teak floors, canopied feather beds, whirlpool tubs, and wood-burning fireplaces. Breakfast can be delivered to your own private courtyard. The barn rooms offer similar luxuries, but with private decks instead.

Simpson House Inn is a perfect spot for a romantic interlude. And for dinner, the most atmospheric restaurants of downtown Santa Barbara are all within walking distance.

SIMPSON HOUSE INN

Telephone: **(800) 676-1280; (805) 963-7067; fax (805) 564-4811**
Address: **121 East Arrellaga Street, Santa Barbara 93101**
Rates: **$110 to $235, including afternoon wine, hors d'oeuvres, and full breakfast**
Directions: **From US-101, exit at Mission Street; proceed north six blocks to Anacapa Street and turn right, then left on Arrellaga Street.**

El Encanto

No matter where you stay in Santa Barbara, a sunset drink at El Encanto Hotel is not to be missed. From the hillside terrace you can see all of Santa Barbara and the sparkling Pacific. Since opening its doors in 1915, El Encanto has been a landmark retreat, drawing the likes of Franklin Roosevelt and Hedy Lamarr. Although the Spanish bungalow rooms are fairly conventional, the ten acres of gardens are quite romantic—especially the lily pond area, encircled by a profusion of greenery and flowers. Inviting lawn swings add to the languorous air.

EL ENCANTO

Telephone: **(800) 346-7039; (805) 687-5000; fax (805) 687-3903**
Address: **1900 Lasuen Road, Santa Barbara 93103**
Rates: **$160 to $660, breakfast included Sunday through Thursday**
Directions: **From US-101, exit at Mission Street and head north; turn left on Laguna Street and right on Los Olivos Street past the mission; turn right on Alameda Padre Serra and left on Lasuen Road.**

St. Mary's Retreat House

Just around the corner from the Santa Barbara Mission is St. Mary's Retreat House, a small convent run by the Sisters of the Holy Nativity. The atmosphere is fairly religious, but being an Episcopalian is not prerequisite to staying here. Men and women of all denominations are welcome for a quiet retreat. Because most weekends are taken up with groups, the best chance for individuals is on weekdays.

At St. Mary's Retreat House, people of all denominations are welcome for a quiet retreat.

Although a group of giggling teenagers was in residence when I visited, Sister Barbara Jean told me the nuns usually maintain a monastic silence in the house. The guest rooms are small and spartan, with curtains in place of doors.

The Tudor-style house is handsome, but what I liked best about St. Mary's was its lovely terrace. Facing the hills of Santa Barbara, it overlooks seven acres of convent grounds that run down to the creek. And if that isn't enough spiritual beauty for you, just stroll over to the mission, one of the finest in California.

ST. MARY'S RETREAT HOUSE

Telephone: **(805) 682-4117**
Address: **505 East Los Olivos, Santa Barbara 93105.**
Rate: **$60, including all meals**
Directions: **From US-101, exit at Mission Street and head north; turn left at Laguna Street and right on Los Olivos just past the mission.**

LITTLE NOVELTY: Like big romantic bathrooms? Try the Blueberry Room at **The Bayberry Inn** in Santa Barbara. Light-filled and white-tiled, it's like a sitting room, with a full sofa next to the large clawfoot tub. The rest of the inn has a pleasant, post-Victorian elegance, intimate garden, and gracious innkeepers. But the main reason I would stay here is for the Blueberry bathroom. For more information, call (805) 682-3199.

Four Seasons Biltmore

Whenever I bring first-time visitors to Santa Barbara, I always begin by swinging over to the Four Seasons Biltmore. Framed by palms, eucalyptus trees, and expansive lawns, this grand old dame has reigned for decades as one of the most dignified Spanish-style hotels in California. The rooms, resort facilities, and amenities are exactly as one would expect of a fine hotel. It's the pervasive Old California aura that makes it stand out. You can feel it when you enter the lobby with its heavy wood-beamed ceiling and terra cotta floors; you can feel it when you stroll the extensive grounds of freshly cut lawns and bungalow-style cottages.

The Odell Cottage is a misnomer if ever I heard one. The "cottage" contains three huge bedrooms, four bathrooms, a thirty-five-foot salon, and private patio. Among its many luxuries, the master shower has a foot-level faucet so you can check the water temperature before stepping in.

The Four Seasons Resorts updated the Biltmore in recent years, and I was disappointed by two changes. The cocktail lounge still has its lovely arched picture window facing the Pacific, but the decor has been too formalized. Worse than that, their legendary Sunday brunches are now a whopping forty dollars per person! I remember going there with my family when it cost twelve dollars. It was a splurge then, but it's nearly prohibitive now.

FOUR SEASONS BILTMORE

Telephone: **(800) 332-3442; (805) 969-2261; fax (805) 969-4682**
Address: **1260 Channel Drive, Santa Barbara 93108**
Rates: **$199 to $1,700**
Directions: **From US-101, exit at Olive Mill Drive, and head toward the ocean.**

Immaculate Heart Center for Spiritual Renewal and La Casa de Maria

The Immaculate Heart Center for Spiritual Renewal is one of the most beautiful settings you'll ever see for a retreat destination. Located right next to the San Ysidro Ranch in Montecito, the entry is lined by a splendid tunnel of overhanging trees. The twenty-six acres of grounds are naturally landscaped with native oaks and pathways curling here and there. It's extremely tranquil and soothing. Only the sounds of birds and a creek running through the property distract you. Little benches, statues, and private nooks are tucked everywhere. The center itself, where guests stay, is a twenties stone estate house that looks like a European villa. (Indeed, the property was once a private estate.) They have only six rooms which, of course, book very quickly.

The center is operated by the Immaculate Heart Community, a Roman Catholic order of women who have over the last century evolved into a lay community of single and married Christians. They welcome anyone—individuals and couples "whatever their journey"—for a time of gentle silence and personal retreat. Dinner is served family style, while breakfast and lunch can be picked up any time.

Sharing the same grounds with Immaculate Heart is a larger retreat center called La Casa de Maria. The only catch, however, is that you must be part of an organized retreat program to stay here. Their programs last only a few days and deal with a wide range of subjects, ranging from Zen meditation to sensory awareness to spiritual subjects. If you can't get a room at Immaculate Heart Center, La Casa de Maria is a viable alternative. Their accommodations, housed in several buildings, range from private rooms to dormitory bunk beds.

Regardless of which center you stay in, this is one of the least formal religious retreats in California. The first time I came here, I expected to see a demure nun at the reception desk. Instead, I was greeted by the center's tanned, athletic-looking male masseuse, who was filling in. While wandering the grounds, I was further surprised to see tennis courts and a swimming pool. The religious focus is very low-key compared to most retreats. For a first-time retreat, Immaculate Heart Center would be a wonderful choice.

Booking a room at Immaculate Heart Center is a bit different from the usual procedure. If you want to stay anytime during the months of September, October, and November, you must call on August 1 for reservations; for December, January, and February, call on November 1. And so on.

IMMACULATE HEART CENTER FOR SPIRITUAL RENEWAL

Telephone: **(805) 969-2474**
Address: **888 San Ysidro Lane, Santa Barbara 93108**
Suggested
donation: **$45 for individuals, $55 for married couples, including all meals. Open Wednesday through Sunday only.**
Directions: **From US-101 in Montecito, exit at San Ysidro Road and head north; turn right on East Valley Road and left on El Bosque Road.**

LA CASA DE MARIA

Telephone: **(805) 969-5031; fax (805) 969-2759**
Address: **800 El Bosque Road, Santa Barbara 93108**
Rates: **vary depending on program**
Directions: **same as Immaculate Heart Center.**

San Ysidro Ranch

Who hasn't heard of the San Ysidro Ranch? Open since 1893, this marvelous, 540-acre setting has long been a favorite hideaway of celebrities. Lawrence Olivier and Vivien Leigh were married here. John and Jacqueline Kennedy honeymooned here. What greater credentials could you ask for?

After finally visiting the Ranch myself, I was surprised by how unpretentious it is. Despite all the rich and famous guests who are served, the staff is genuinely warm and open with everyone. Their informality (the cat asleep on the lounge couch) and personal touches (labeling each guest cottage with the names of its occupants in wood block letters) set it apart from other luxury hotels.

Also surprising—the Ranch welcomes pets, and will supply everything from pet beds to special, vitamin-fortified doggy water in the cottages. At the front desk is a pet registration book and bubble gum machine filled with dog kibbles. The registration book shows names such as Bruno, Duchess, and Rupert. One guest who went by the alias of Big Al listed Poochums as his dog. Under the type of pet, he wrote "Bad Ass."

The grounds are delightful. The terraced, oak- and sycamore-covered property has a real vintage California feel. Scattered along the hillside are horse stables, a bocce court, herb and vegetable garden, wedding garden, and rustic Stonehouse Restaurant (rated by *Conde Nast Traveler* as one of the top fifty restaurants in the country).

All the single-story cottages have distinct personalities and a fresh country glow. Most cottages are distinguished by wood floors, beamed ceilings, wood stoves, and crisp, white, down comforters on the beds. The accommodations are both elegant and rustic—a hard balance to maintain.

My favorite cottages are those with decks overlooking San Ysidro Creek and its barranca. The Willow Tree Suite, for instance, is absolutely stunning. Decorated with the utmost taste, it has a big, beautiful living room with fireplace, all the luxuries one could ask for, and a hot tub on a private creek-side deck. Except for the $750 price tag, it doesn't get any better than this.

SAN YSIDRO RANCH

Telephone: **(800) 368-6788; fax (805) 565-1995**
Address: **900 San Ysidro Lane, Santa Barbara 93108**
Rates: **$235 to $750; pets welcome**
Directions: **From US-101 in Montecito, exit at San Ysidro Road and head north to San Ysidro Lane.**

White Lotus Foundation

White Lotus Foundation is a modest retreat center that clings to a steep, rustic hillside in the San Marcos Pass. Through the narrow mountain pass you have an excellent view of the distant ocean and Channel Islands. Accommodations are basic, ranging from sleeping spaces in an open loft above the common reading room, to yurts and campsites terraced down the hillside. Most people bring their own food and cook in the community kitchen.

The main focus here is yoga—in-depth weekend and week-long programs designed for every level, beginning yoga to teacher certification. Although it's program-oriented, individuals can spend the night here on a personal retreat and use all of the facilities—hike, have a massage, swim in the creek, meditate, or read in the light, airy library. Overnighters can also enroll in whatever yoga classes are offered that day.

The five yurts (a good choice for privacy) are nestled among the trees at different levels on a steep dirt pathway. Each yurt has a tiny outdoor deck, wood floor and canvas-covered wood frame, skylit roof, futons (bring your own bedding), a heater, and a few other basics. You can get all the exercise your heart desires just trekking up the hill from your yurt to the community building. I never ventured farther down the hill to the campsites and creek, fearing it would take me half the day to get back up.

While the yoga is a special draw, White Lotus is a tranquil, unpretentious spot for just communing with nature without the discomforts of bare-bones camping. As the brochure puts it: "The inquiry into enlightened living has traditionally been shared in retreat in powerful, natural settings."

WHITE LOTUS FOUNDATION

Telephone: **(805) 964-1944**
Address: **2500 San Marcos Pass, Santa Barbara 93105**
Rates: **$35 per person; inquire about yoga programs**
Directions: **From US-101 north, take SR-154 for about six miles to 2529 (a large white mailbox on the left).**

Mount Calvary Monastery and Retreat House

If ever there was an ethereal setting for a monastery, it's at Mount Calvary Monastery and Retreat House. Perched on one of the highest ridges above Santa Barbara, this Spanish-style retreat house has a stupendous ocean panorama. Because the ridge it clings to is so narrow, expect a case of vertigo while driving the last stretch. But from up here, on top of the world, one feels removed from all earthly concerns.

Mount Calvary was founded in 1947 for the Order of the Holy Cross, an Episcopal monastic community in the Benedictine tradition. Individuals and groups of men and women of all religious denominations are welcome. A private, individual retreat can be arranged for one to several days. One of the main functions of this retreat house is to provide a place of quiet withdrawal from the distractions of ordinary life. Solitude, silence, meditations, discussions, and reading are some of the reasons people come here. Guests are also welcome, but not required, to participate in four daily services. A ringing bell announces chapel services and meals. At 8:30 each evening, the carpet rolls up and the doors are locked. Before descending back down into the real world, you're expected to clean and prepare your room for the next guest.

MOUNT CALVARY MONASTERY AND RETREAT HOUSE

Telephone: **(805) 962-9855 (Monday through Friday)**
  Address: **2500 Mount Calvary Road, P.O. Box 1296, Santa Barbara 93105, open Monday afternoon to Saturday afternoon**
Suggested donation (but no one is turned away for lack of funds): **$50 per person for the first night; $45 for each subsequent night, including meals; reservations required**
Directions: **From US-101, exit at Mission Street. Turn left on Laguna Street, wind past the mission, and turn right on Mountain Drive, which makes a sharp left at one point. At the fork, take Gibraltar Road up the mountain to the Mount Calvary sign on the left.**

SOLVANG

The Chimney Sweep Inn

On the face of it, Solvang is a gold mine. The Danish village is full of wonderful, half-timbered buildings and simulated thatched roofs straight from the pages of Hans Christian Andersen. But just as the facades of the Disneyland hotels are only facades, so too is the case with Solvang. No matter how charming they look on the outside, most interiors are utterly conventional. Only one lodging, the Chimney Sweep Inn, carries the storybook theme into its guest rooms.

The Chimney Sweep Inn carries its storybook theme into the guest rooms as well.

The Chimney Sweep Inn was designed as a tribute to C. S. Lewis's *Chronicles of Narnia*. The late Dr. Bill Van Valin, the inn's original owner, loved these stories and worked with an architect to create an inn that would accurately convey the Land of Narnia. The outside results are delightful. A tiny village of half-timbered enchanted cottages with mullioned windows and vine-covered chimneys are snuggled in a grassy, rose-filled garden. Little arched foot bridges (decorated with the spoked wheels of an old rickshaw used for the filming of *The King and I*) lead over a winding brook and lily-pad-covered fish pond. The entry to the garden reads "Welcome to Narnia."

The Dawn Treader and the Tree House are the two most Narnia-like cottages inside. The wood floors are crafted from the planks of an old bridge; the front doors are built of heavy timbers and wrought-iron straps. Hand-painted tilework in the bathrooms, kitchens, and one fireplace depicts scenes from the *Chronicles of Narnia*. The headboard of one bed is fashioned from turn-of-the-century bank teller windows. Books from the *Chronicles* are placed in each cottage.

All six cottages have a private patio and spa, kitchen, living room with fireplace, and king bed with down comforter. There are more rooms and suites in the main lodge. Like most of the cottages, their decor is tastefully traditional but less elaborate.

Any child would love this inn. If you bring children here the week before Easter, they can enjoy the storytelling at Solvang's annual fairy tale festival.

THE CHIMNEY SWEEP INN

Telephone:	**(800) 824-6444; (805) 688-2111**
Address:	**1554 Copenhagen Drive, Solvang 93463**
Rates:	**$70 to $255, including continental breakfast**
Directions:	**From US-101, exit at SR-246 to Solvang; turn right on Atterdag Road and right on Copenhagen Drive.**

The Alisal Guest Ranch and Resort

The Alisal Guest Ranch and Resort, just south of Solvang, has been a guest ranch since 1946 and a working cattle ranch as well.

In fact, guests who are experienced riders can join in periodic half-day cattle drives and accompany the wranglers across the ranch into the corrals. The drive is capped off by a chuck-wagon lunch of barbecued meats and homemade buttermilk biscuits.

The guest ranch is unique for other reasons. For one thing, it's a horse-lovers' paradise. Eighty to one hundred horses are available for guided rides over the ten-thousand-acre property. Morning rides begin with campfire breakfasts of flapjacks and a cowboy poetry recital. Moonlit rides to the resort's private lake end with dinner barbecues under the stars. Anyone, including beginners from the age of seven on, can take riding clinics.

There's also a full range of activities for children at the ranch—hayrides, sing-alongs, arts and crafts, and storytelling, plus lessons in tennis, golf, sailing, and windsurfing on the resort's lake. Small riders can participate in mini-rodeos and learn about roping and animal grooming.

With events like reptile roundups, bingo, and sing-alongs, one might expect this guest ranch to be fairly rustic. It's not. The lawns are manicured, the golf course and tennis courts are top-notch, and jackets are required of men for dinner. The ranch-style guest cottages are well appointed and comfortable. A podunk place this is not.

THE ALISAL GUEST RANCH AND RESORT

Telephone: **(800) 4-ALISAL; (805) 688-6411; fax (805) 688-2510**
Address: **1054 Alisal Road, Solvang 93463**
Rates: **$295 to $380, including breakfast and dinner; two-night minimum requirement**
Directions: **From US-101 at Buellton, exit at SR-246 and head east to Solvang; turn right on Alisal Road.**

ZACA LAKE

Zaca Lake Resort

Even though it's less than fifteen miles off Highway 101, Zaca Lake Resort has the feel of being incredibly remote. It must have

Zaca Lake Resort is on the only natural lake in Santa Barbara County.

been those last five miles of bumpy dirt road that did it for me. Oh, and the four or five streams I had to ford in my rental car: They were just shallow little streams, but this was in the summertime. I wonder how deep they get in the spring?

Once you finally reach Zaca Lake, however, it's worth the drive. The small lake—the only natural lake in Santa Barbara County—is a refreshing blue green, with just a few boats floating about lazily. (Swimming, but no fishing, is allowed.) A lodge facing the lake houses the reception office and a simple restaurant. Seventeen individual cabins, which are set slightly back from the lake, accommodate anywhere from two to twenty-two people. Built in the thirties and forties, the cabins are less rustic than they appear from the outside, with big stone fireplaces (wood is supplied), and unusually nice bathrooms with large Jacuzzi tubs. However, none of the units, except the group cabin, have kitchens or refrigerators. This forces most guests to eat in the somewhat overpriced restaurant.

The resort, which also goes by the name of Human Potential Foundation, was created by Gerald Kessler, who purchased it with his son in the mid-eighties. Their goal is to make the resort as self-sufficient as possible, generating solar and methane-powered energy and growing all their own vegetables. They couldn't have chosen a more peaceful site. Surrounding the lake is the pine- and oak-filled Los Padres National Forest with the gentle San Rafael Mountains all around. Hiking is the main activity here. They also have rowboat and canoe rentals. But judging from what I saw, lazing quietly around the lake is the greatest lure,

ZACA LAKE RESORT

Telephone:	**(805) 688-4891**
Address:	**P.O. Box 187, Los Olivos 93441**
Rates:	**$90 to $400**
Directions:	**From US-101, exit at Zaca Station Road and veer left on Foxen Canyon Road. After three and one-half miles, look for entrance to the road to Zaca on the right. The last five miles are dirt.**

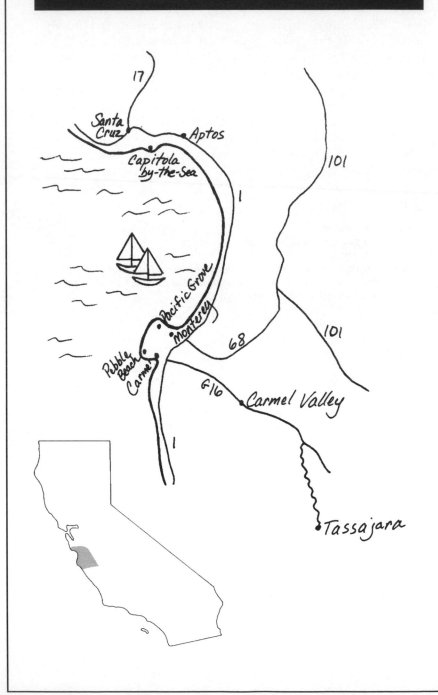

MONTEREY BAY AREA

Mangels House

The approach to Mangels House is truly beautiful, with old Monterey pines and cypress trees lining the driveway. The sprawling 1880s house is situated on four acres of lawns and gardens. It also borders a ten thousand-acre park of redwoods, ferns, creeks, and trails. Although it's less than a mile from Monterey Bay, the property has a thoroughly secluded feel.

Innkeepers Jacqueline and Ron Fisher spent two years in Zaire and have decorated one of their spacious, airy guest rooms with artifacts from Africa. Named after their son, Nicholas, the room features masks and dolls representing tribal witch doctors. Its floors are laid with woven raffia mats. Some of the other rooms are surprisingly un-Victorian, as well.

Even non-avid hikers find themselves drawn into the woods that surround the Mangels House. Guests often set out for hikes after breakfast, supplied with a picnic lunch and trail maps.

MANGELS HOUSE

Telephone:	**(408) 688-7982**
Address:	**570 Aptos Creek Road, P.O. Box 302, Aptos 95001**
Rates:	**$105 to $135, including full breakfast and evening sherry**
Directions:	**From Highway 1, exit at Seacliff-Aptos and head inland; turn right on Soquel Drive and left on Aptos Creek Road.**

The Inn at Depot Hill offers luxury and romance.

CAPITOLA-BY-THE-SEA

The Inn at Depot Hill

Of the hundreds of bed and breakfasts I've seen in California, few top the luxury of the Inn at Depot Hill. This is a destination inn—the kind of place you check into and never want to leave.

Formerly a 1901 train depot, the historic building was totally transformed by Suzie Lankes and her partner, Dan Floyd. The only physical reminder of its former days are the front bay windows where passengers once purchased their tickets. But in keeping with the travel theme, each of the eight guest rooms is designed to evoke a different romantic destination. At a table in the dining room-reception area is a clever trompe l'oeil scene that depicts the dining car of a train.

No matter which guest room you select, you can't lose. Being partial to blue and white, I found the Dutch-inspired Delft Room most visually pleasing. Its feather bed is canopied in crisp Battenburg lace. But I wound up staying in Sissinghurst, which fulfilled all of my Anglophile fantasies with its traditional English garden chintz decor. Stratford-on-Avon is also very British, with its cabbage rose patterns and a particularly inviting window seat. There's the Paris Room, swathed in black and white French toile, as well as Portofino, Cote D'Azur, and Capitola. The Railroad Baron's Room is decorated like a sumptuous vintage pullman, with a domed ceiling, thick, deep-red and gold fabrics, and ornate moldings.

When it comes to amenities, no expense has been spared. Each bedroom has a wood-burning fireplace, two televisions (a little one is in the bathroom), built-in stereo system, VCR (with a library of videos concealed behind Shakespeare faux book covers in the parlor), telephone and modem, long-stemmed roses, and fluffy feather bed. Every day the embroidered linens (including the duvet cover) are washed and ironed. Most of the suites have private patios with outdoor hot tubs under a gazebo—very romantic at night. Each marble bathroom features a two-person shower, piles of Egyptian cotton towels, hair dryer, bottled water, luxury soaps, coffee maker, marble ice bucket, makeup remover, wine glasses, close-up mirror, and even a lint remover.

Each afternoon, wine, Italian sodas, and hors d'oeuvres are served on the dining room buffet. After dinner, they're replaced by dessert and port. Breakfast, which is artfully presented, can be delivered to your room or the patio.

Anyone seeking an incredibly romantic, indulgent interlude should put the Inn at Depot Hill high on their list.

THE INN AT DEPOT HILL

Telephone:	**(800) 57-B AND B; (408) 462-DEPO; fax (408) 462-3697**
Address:	**250 Monterey Avenue, Capitola-by-the-Sea 95010**
Rates:	**$165 to $250, including full breakfast, afternoon wine and hors d'oeuvres, and dessert**
Directions:	**From Highway 1 in Capitola, exit at Park Avenue/New Brighton Beach and head toward the ocean; turn left on Monterey Avenue and immediately left into the inn's driveway.**

CARMEL

Mission Ranch

Mission Ranch, which has a well-known proprietor by the name of Clint Eastwood, is most remarkable for its serene setting. Located right next to the Carmel Mission, this sizable spread is perched on a bluff overlooking a green meadow of grazing sheep that seems to stretch endlessly to the ocean. Adirondack chairs practically beg one to sink in and soak up the scenery.

The guest quarters are equally atmospheric in an Old California way. The Ranch was a working dairy farm until it opened its doors to lodgers in the thirties. Some original buildings have been converted into guest quarters. Nestled among the towering eucalyptus, cypress trees, and Monterey pines, the accommodations include a restored farmhouse, barn, bunkhouse, hay loft, and 1900 honeymoon cottage once used in the film *Summer Place*. The former creamery is now the Ranch's restaurant, a popular watering hole for locals and Mr. Eastwood, too, when he's in town.

More guest rooms with private balconies in several newer buildings face the meadow. Like the historic buildings, they're all decorated in an unfrilly manner, with patchwork quilts and American country furnishings. Every building has its own personality. But the 1850s farmhouse, with colorful geraniums dripping from window boxes, looks mighty inviting.

MISSION RANCH

Telephone: **(800) 538-8221; (408) 624-6436; fax (408) 626-4163**
Address: **26270 Dolores Street, Carmel 93923**
Rates: **$85 to 225, including "continental plus" breakfast**
Directions: **From Highway 1, exit at Rio Road and head west; just past the Carmel Mission, turn left on Lasuen Drive.**

Cypress Inn

The Cypress Inn is going to the dogs: Not only are pets accepted, but they're welcomed with open arms and dog biscuits. Co-owned by animal rights activist Doris Day, this small hotel encourages guests to bring their pets—a policy that draws an average of three pets a night and a loyal clientele. It's not uncommon to see people registering with (mostly) dogs of all sizes. The friendly staff provides pet beds, litter boxes, food, and even pet sitters upon request. The living room even features a "family photo album" of furry regulars. There is one stipulation—your pet can't be left unattended in a guest room. Once when some guests ignored this rule and left the room, their dog somehow managed to lock the door latch. A staff member climbed up a ladder to gain access, only to find that the dog wouldn't let him in. His owner finally had to scale the ladder himself.

The Moorish Mediterranean style twenties hotel has a narrow but pretty courtyard where many weddings are held. One uniquely shaped room has a bed tucked up a spiral staircase inside the main tower of the building. Called the Tower Room, this little bedroom is quite cozy, with book nooks, original tilework, and a view of Carmel. Near the lobby, there's a bar decorated with old Doris Day movie posters. Otherwise, the remaining guest rooms and common areas are thoroughly conventional.

CYPRESS INN

Telephone: **(800) 443-7443; (408) 624-3871; fax (408) 624-8216**
Address: **Lincoln and Seventh Streets, P.O. Box Y, Carmel 93921**
Rates: **$95 to $245, including continental breakfast; each pet $17 extra**
Directions: **From Highway 1, exit at Ocean Avenue and turn left on Lincoln Street.**

Lamp Lighter Inn

The distinct Carmel charm of Lamp Lighter Inn makes it impossible to leave it out of this book. The pink brochure, filled with exclamation marks, says, "We have elves who play in our gardens and they will be here to welcome you!" Situated on the main drag of town, the inn consists of several storybook cottages with Dutch doors and simulated thatched roofs. The courtyard is filled with flowers and tree ferns. The guest rooms have sugary names such as Katydid and Blue Bird. The Hansel and Gretel Cottage looked most comfortable with a living room, wood-burning fireplace, and small, extra loft above the bedroom. Nothing fancy, but they certainly get an "A" for enthusiasm.

LAMP LIGHTER INN

Telephone:	**(408) 624-7372**
Address:	**Ocean Avenue and Camino Real, P.O. Box 604, Carmel 93921-0604**
Rates:	**$100 to $160, including breakfast at a nearby restaurant**
Directions:	**From Highway 1, exit at Ocean Avenue.**

CARMEL VALLEY

Stonepine

How would you like to step into a Ralph Lauren fantasy? Visit Stonepine, an exclusive 330-acre estate in the Carmel Valley. Built in 1930 by the Crocker banking family, it is the oldest working thoroughbred racing farm west of the Mississippi. Its seclusion and elite sense of privacy are so well protected that many celebrities have been married here. Those who come here do so to rest and be pampered.

Getting here is half the fun. If you want the full treatment, you can fly a chartered helicopter from the Monterey Airport to

Stonepine's Phantom V Rolls Royce is available to pick you up.

the estate, or arrange to be picked up in a creamy Phantom V Rolls Royce. After a twenty-minute drive into the rolling hills of the Carmel Valley, the electronic gates of Stonepine swing open. A seemingly endless driveway meanders over the estate to a French country-style villa known as Chateau Noel. Pierre Rolin, your handsome concierge, is the epitome of European sophistication. As he leads you from one exquisite room to another, he points out that the columns supporting the loggia are from ancient Rome; that the oak paneling in the library and dining room is from nineteenth-century France; and that the carved limestone fireplace in the living room dates from nineteenth-century Italy. It's like touring a priceless museum, except you get to stay here.

You can choose from eight suites in the chateau (named after designers such as Chanel and Cartier) or four slightly less formal suites in the Paddock House of the equestrian center. There's also the Briar Rose Cottage, which has two bedrooms, a dining room, and living room with stone fireplace. Or, you can have the whole estate to yourself for a mere ten thousand dollars a night.

If you care to tour the grounds, do so by horse-drawn carriage. The equestrian center has an impressive collection of carriages, among them a Roman chariot. Winding paths lead you past expansive gardens, a polo field, archery range, tennis courts, soccer field, and croquet lawn. Serious equestrians can show off their horsemanship in a hunter-jumping course, dressage arena, or four-furlong sulky track.

The cuisine, nothing short of gourmet, is served on Limoges and Royal Crown Derby china, with sterling silver and Waterford crystal. You can have your breakfast in the loggia among the old olive trees or on the wisteria-covered terrace overlooking soft lawns that slope down to the swimming pool. This must be as luxurious as life on earth gets.

STONEPINE

Telephone:	**(408) 659-2245; fax (400) 059-5160**
Address:	**150 East Carmel Valley Road, Carmel Valley 93924**
Rates:	**$225 to $750, including continental breakfast**
Directions:	**From Highway 1, head east on Carmel Valley Road for thirteen and one-half miles.**

Tassajara

A century ago, visitors came to Tassajara by horse, or they walked the last fourteen miles of dirt trails on an arduous journey that took two days. Although the trail has since been expanded to a dirt road and the trip can now be made by car, it still takes two hours to reach Tassajara from Carmel Valley Village. Those fourteen miles of hairpin curves (especially the last half hour, when you are con-stantly riding your brake) are notoriously tortuous—so tortuous, in fact, that many people leave their cars in Jamesburg and ride the once-a-day van in (for an extra thirty-five dollars round-trip).

Like the Green Gulch Farm Zen Center in the Bay Area, Tassajara is now a Buddhist monastery, the first outside of Asia. Each summer, the monastery opens its gates to guests who come to enjoy the Japanese-style hot springs baths and the soothing quiet of the mountains. You can also join residents in meditation, workshops, and other activities. Accommodations include redwood cabins, Japanese-style tatami cabins, yurts, turn-of-the-century stone rooms, and dorm rooms, all of which are lit by kerosene lamps (there is no electricity). The family-style meals are vegetarian.

Because of its remoteness, Tassajara is one of two places listed in this book that I have yet to visit. But if people have been going to such lengths to reach it for the past one hundred years, it must be special.

TASSAJARA

Telephone: **(415) 431-3771**
Reservations: **300 Page Street, San Francisco 94102**
Rates: **$67 to $130 per person, double; $77 to $200 per person, single; all meals included**
Directions: **two hours southeast of Carmel Valley; call or write for instructions.**

MONTEREY

Old Monterey Inn

The Old Monterey Inn has a moodiness that best typifies the darkly wooded, misty atmosphere of the Monterey Peninsula. Set away from town in a quiet residential neighborhood, its enchanted gardens are filled with gnarled oak trees, ferns, and hanging flower pots with whimsically decorated faces.

The most unique room of this English Tudor-style bed and breakfast is the Library, a dreamy haven of book-lined walls. It has a large stone fireplace and bed surrounded by windows that look out to the twisted old oak trees. Another room, Serengeti, features an African safari theme, with antique travel mementos and a bed swathed in mosquito netting.

OLD MONTEREY INN

Telephone: **(800) 350-2344; (408) 375-8284; fax (408) 375-6730**
Address: **500 Martin Street, Monterey 93940**
Rates: **$170 to $240, including full breakfast, afternoon tea, and evening hors d'oeuvres**
Directions: **From Highway 1, exit at Munras Avenue, turn left on Pacific Street and left on Martin Street.**

The Jabberwock

> 'Twas brillig and the slithy toves
> Did gyre and gimble in the wabe,
> All mimsy were the borogroves,
> And the mome raths outgrabe.
> —Lewis Carroll, from "The Jabberwocky"

When you call the Jabberwock, you might get a recording that says, "We're out chasing the white rabbit." This is only a taste of the looking-glass journey you will experience at this *Alice in Wonderland*-inspired inn. For instance, your welcome note has to be held up to a mirror to be read; some of the clocks are backward; guest rooms have names such as Mimsey and Wabe, Brillig and Borogrove; the common telephone is kept in a little alcove called the Burbling Room; and the evening wine is accompanied by (what else?) Cheshire cheese.

Breakfasts at the Jabberwock are a real performance. Innkeeper Jim Allen, a storyteller who reads to local school children, captivates guests with stories while they savor their snorkleberry flumptious (cheese blintz) or phantasmagoria (it's a surprise). Ceazur, their English bull terrier, is another resident personality who will, upon command, perform a nifty trick with the dog-treat-filled gum ball machine at the entry.

Although this bed and breakfast might sound really wacky, it is actually quite tame. Once a Victorian-era convent, all guest and common rooms are traditionally Victorian in decor, with almost no evidence of the *Alice* theme in the bedrooms or gardens.

THE JABBERWOCK

Telephone: **(408) 372-4777**
Address: **598 Laine Street, Monterey 93940**
Rates: **$100 to $185, including full breakfast and afternoon wine and hors d'oeuvres**
Directions: **From Highway 1, exit at SR-68 west to Pacific Grove/Pebble Beach; after two and one-half miles, turn right on Prescott, then right on Pine Street, and left on Hoffman Avenue to Laine Street.**

PACIFIC GROVE

The Green Gables Inn

With its fanciful Queen Anne architecture and multiple gables, the Green Gables Inn is a traffic stopper. The inn is ideally situated across from Monterey Bay and its rocky, dramatic shoreline. Built in the 1880s for the mistress of a prominent businessman, this ornate Victorian was also the sixties home of Roger and Sally Post. They now own a whole collection of well-run bed and breakfasts called the Four Sisters Inns (named after their four daughters). Like the other Four Sisters Inns, Green Gables has its trademark teddy bears everywhere, an original carousel horse at the entry, and a host of amenities—full breakfast, afternoon wine and hors d'oeuvres, all-day goodies, and evening turn-down service. The other two closest Four Sisters Inns—the Gosby House and Cobblestone Inn—are equally yuppified, but Green Gables has the most character.

There is a newer carriage house in back, but I prefer the upstairs rooms in the main house—especially the Chapel Room,

The fancy architecture, including gables, makes the Green Gables Inn a special attraction.

with its rib-vaulted ceiling, mullioned windows, and window seat overlooking the bay.

THE GREEN GABLES INN

Telephone: **(800) 722-1774 or (408) 375-2095; fax (408) 375-5437**
Address: **104 Fifth Street, Pacific Grove 93950**
Rates: **$100 to $160, including full breakfast and afternoon wine and hors d'oeuvres**
Directions: **From Highway 1, exit at SR-68 to Pacific Grove/Pebble Beach; after two and one-half miles, turn right on Forest; then right on Ocean View Boulevard.**

PEBBLE BEACH

LITTLE NOVELTY: Every night at sunset, a kilted bagpiper strolls the golf course of **The Inn at Spanish Bay** on the Monterey Peninsula. The Scottish links here are rivaled in beauty only by the golf course of the inn's sister hotel—the **Lodge at Pebble Beach**—down the road. For more information, call the Pebble Beach Resorts at (800) 654-9300 or (408) 647-7500.

SANTA CRUZ

The Babbling Brook Inn

First it was settled by the Ohlone Indians; then it was a gristmill for the mission fathers; by 1877 it was a tannery. From 1909 on, when a log cabin was added, it subsequently served as home to a group of actors, writers, the last representative to the Russian czar, and even a self-declared Austrian countess. In the forties it was a restaurant, and finally, by 1981, an inn.

The Babbling Brook Inn is certainly not without its colorful past. But I mention the inn because of its lush, enchanted setting. Set around a meandering brook and tiered waterfalls are woodsy shingled chalets nestled in a garden of pines and redwoods. A delicate white gazebo (purchased by innkeeper Helen King from a UC Santa Cruz Shakespearean production) sits amid huge tree ferns, providing a romantic spot for weddings.

A covered footbridge, brick footpath, and stone steps lead up to the much-expanded main building—a rambling, California craftsman structure that houses several guest rooms, a living room, and a breakfast room. But most of the guest quarters are in the two-story chalets. Named after famous impressionist painters such as Monet, Van Gogh, and Cezanne, the country French-inspired bedrooms have Franklin fireplaces, private balconies, and rockers overlooking the tranquil garden.

It's hard to believe this inn is right in Santa Cruz, less than a mile from the boardwalk—home of California's only surviving wooden roller coaster. I'm not a big roller coaster fan, but this one is a blast.

THE BABBLING BROOK INN

Telephone: **(800) 866-1131; (408) 427-2437; fax (408) 427-2457**
Address: **1025 Laurel Street, Santa Cruz 95060**
Rates: **$85 to $265, including full breakfast and evening wine and cheese**
Directions: **From Highway 1 (Mission Street), exit at Laurel Street and head toward the ocean.**

5 SAN FRANCISCO BAY AREA

Captain Walsh House

By the time I arrived at the Captain Walsh House, I was at the tail end of an exhausting guidebook deadline. I'd covered and photographed twenty-two bed and breakfasts in eleven days, and this was the last one. I was flagging; anxious to get home. But seeing this inn was like a shot in the arm. After one night there, I felt renewed and completely re-inspired. When I finally, reluctantly, went home, I couldn't stop gushing to my friends about this exciting place.

The Captain Walsh House has the most inspired interior of any bed and breakfast I've seen in California. It's a daring labor of love, created by architect Reed Robbins and her husband, Steve. Together, they transformed this rundown 1849 home into a sumptuous space that positively glows with energy. They tossed all the usual decorating ideas right out their Gothic windows. The results are totally original, unpredictable, and "quirky," as Reed calls it.

Take the main salon, for instance. The wood floors have been painted a pale yellow with black diamond patterns. The walls are also the palest of pale. Rich, ivory-colored fabrics are gathered in random folds on the center table. Gauzy, Medieval-style drapes hang at the tall windows. Dark, Gothic gargoyles, candelabras, mirrors, and church relics contrast with the salon's creamy background, more whimsical than somber in such a romantic setting. Throughout most of the house there's this delicious theme of the Gothic and Medieval touches against a backdrop of creamy white, pale yellow, and pink.

Across the hall, in a smaller salon, the walls appear to have vertically striped wallpaper. Upon closer inspection, you'll see that it's a faux finish—every stripe has been meticulously handpainted, and the thinnest line turns out to be a strip of black tape.

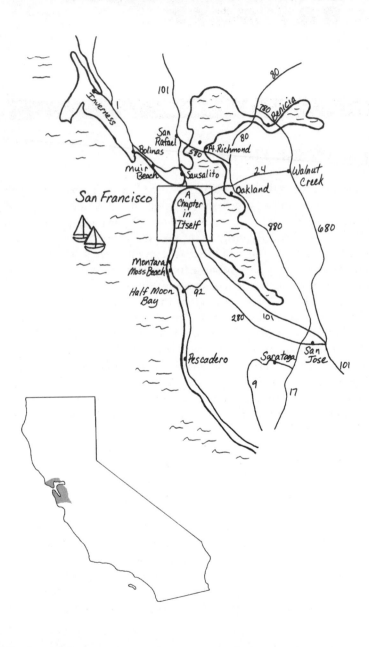

The pillows are piled seven deep on the canopied bed in Epiphania's Room at the Captain Walsh House.

Upstairs, in Epiphania's Room (which was featured on the cover of *Better Homes and Gardens*), the splendid canopied bed sits in the center of the room, its pillows piled seven layers deep. On either side table are Staffordshire Pekingese dog lamps. In the same room is a twenty-four-carat-gold clawfoot tub that looks like it's out of *Alice in Wonderland*. The vaulted ceilings are oddly reminiscent of a church interior. The whole magnificent room is filled with a soft golden light, both from the tall Gothic window and a delicate mix of yellow and pink finish on the walls. When you open the cupboards, you'll find little surprises—I won't say what. I adore Epiphania's Room.

Of the five bedrooms, the most imaginative is the Library, accessed via a narrow flight of stairs off the kitchen. The cozy room is lined with shelves filled with books, goofy trophies, and even a stuffed armadillo. A ladder leads up to a reading loft, with a zebra-skin rug covering not the floor, but the vaulted ceiling instead. The Murphy bed, which is folded down at night, is concealed behind a wall of faux-painted books. Reed and Steve came up here with a glass of wine one night during the restoration process and made up their own cryptic titles for all the faux books, naming their own friends as the authors. For example,

Dangerous Liaisons pays homage to one of their girlfriends who has the worst luck with men; *Stress for Success,* for another acquaintance who is always behind in her work.

Although she has never done interior decorating, Reed has a natural sense of what works and what doesn't—a perfect balance of humor and good taste. Tootling into downtown Benicia in their '61 Dodge, she haunts the thrift shops for new finds— a cat gargoyle for the hallway, or perhaps a cribbage game for one of their favorite guests. As luxuriant as it looks, the whole inn was put together on a shoestring budget. Reed and Steve did all of the hand painting, furniture refinishing, sewing of duvet covers, and window treatments. Whenever they host weddings, which is quite often, they handle everything themselves, from the catering to the flowers to the ceremony. Yet they never seem hurried or stressed out. They have a synergy that is quite special.

Even Bill, their clumber spaniel, is unlike any other resident dog I've encountered. An extremely rare breed, he's a lumbering, bulky, comical white dog who purrs and snores more loudly than any human being I know. Says Reed, "We have to place him strategically so he won't keep guests awake with his snoring." Adds Steve, "We've even recorded his snoring because people always say, 'Well, how bad can it be?'" To demonstrate, he played the Bill cassette for me, and the whole room reverberated with snores and snorts. Bill also has his own cat, named B.C. (Bill's Cat), which he feeds and takes care of himself.

Benicia is a well-kept secret in the northeastern corner of the San Francisco Bay area. It's like a blast from the fifties, with a quaint main street, small-town friendliness, and pretty waterfront.

One travel writer whose guidebook I admire has stayed at the Captain Walsh House four times already. She even spent her honeymoon in the Library. I'm not at all surprised. I'd return here in an instant.

CAPTAIN WALSH HOUSE

Telephone: **(707) 747-5653; fax (707) 747-6265**
Address: **235 East L Street, Benicia 94510**
Rates: **$110 to $125, including full breakfast**
Directions: **From I-780, exit at East Second Street/Central Benicia; turn left on East Second Street, then left on L Street.**

SAN FRANCISCO BAY AREA

BOLINAS

Thomas' White House Inn

If you're looking for the turn-off to Bolinas from Highway 1, chances are the sign will be missing. The locals, who have long discouraged tourism, pull it down on a regular basis. I found the turn-off only because there were other drivers, like me, pulled off at the intersection looking around in bewilderment. "Yep," I thought, "this has to be it."

Because of the missing sign and its off-the-beaten track location, Thomas' White House Inn remains a well-kept secret tucked away in a quiet neighborhood of Bolinas. People have discovered its fabulous headland setting only by word of mouth. The all-white New England-style house has a wonderful flowery walkway flanked by lawns sloping down to the ocean. On a clear day you can see all the way to San Francisco and Half Moon Bay beyond.

Owner Jackie Thomas asked me not to reveal all of her inn's quirks because she wants to leave her guests with some surprises. So I won't describe the downstairs bathroom. But remind Jackie to show it to you—it must be seen to be believed.

THOMAS' WHITE HOUSE INN

Telephone: **(415) 868-0279**
Address: **118 Kale Road, P.O. Box 132, Bolinas 94924**
Rates: **$85 to $95, including continental breakfast**
Directions: **From Highway 1, take the Bolinas-Olema Road exit (marked only by its missing sign); turn right on Mesa Road, left on Overlook, right on Elm Road, and left on Kale Road.**

HALF MOON BAY

Mill Rose Inn

As for Mill Rose Inn, I have never seen a bed and breakfast so romantically over the top as this. Built similar to an English

Victorian cottage, it positively oozes with frills and lace and flowers. Flowers are everywhere. They explode in colorful displays from the garden; they're all over the bedrooms in lavish silk arrangements and dried wreaths; they're the subject of every print, tile, and piece of stained glass. It's almost too much for me, but at the same time I can see why the inn is such a popular wedding site—they host at least two ceremonies every weekend. And frilly as they are, the rooms certainly aren't lacking in romantic indulgences—private entrances, feather beds, fireplaces (except in Baroque), Japanese robes, chocolates, liqueurs, and a champagne breakfast in bed, if desired. Also included are afternoon wine and cheese, plus cake and cookies. You can reserve private time in the garden hot tub, enclosed by latticework.

Half Moon Bay is one of the last places left on the West Coast where you can still go horseback riding on the beach unescorted, provided you are experienced (from nearby Seahorse Ranch and Friendly Acres). Now, that's romantic.

MILL ROSE INN

Telephone: **(800) 900-ROSE; (415) 726-9794; fax (415) 726-3031**
Address: **615 Mill Street, Half Moon Bay 94019**
Rates: **$165 to $265, including full breakfast, afternoon wine and cheese, and dessert**
Directions: **From Highway 1, exit at SR-92, turn right on Main Street and right on Mill Street.**

INVERNESS

Blackthorne Inn

Blackthorne Inn is like a vision from an enchanted dream. Set in a virtual rain forest (kept moist by Inverness's constant fog) of giant firs, laurel bays, and oaks, this joyful inn resembles a giant tree house, complete with decks and spiral staircases, stained-glass windows, and skylights.

Lovingly built in the seventies by local craftsmen, its fairytale look is enhanced by the use of many historic materials. The front doors were taken from the Southern Pacific Railroad in San Francisco; the redwood paneling is from a Bay Area ferry building; and the hearthstones are collected from seven different counties.

Of the five guest rooms that span over four stories, two are particularly beguiling. From Overlook, on the third level, you can open a balcony door and look down upon the inn's airy, wood-paneled living room. Perched high at the top is Eagle's Nest, an octagonal room enclosed by glass, with a 360-degree view of the sky and trees. There's a private sun deck on the roof if you care to brave the ladder. To reach your bathroom, you cross a skybridge to the hot tub deck on the same level. It's wonderfully quirky.

And if you want to reach the driveway from the main level, take a shortcut and slide down the fire pole.

BLACKTHORNE INN

Telephone:	**(415) 663-8621**
Address:	**266 Vallejo Avenue, P.O. Box 712, Inverness 94937**
Rates:	**$105 to $185, including full breakfast**
Directions:	**From Highway 1, take Sir Francis Drake Boulevard toward Inverness; before reaching town, turn left on Vallejo Avenue.**

Manka's Inverness Lodge

Built as a hunting lodge in 1917, Manka's Inverness Lodge is rich in character. It strikes just the right balance between rusticity and luxury. In fact, the whole lodge looks like an ideal setting for an Abercrombie & Fitch catalog.

The main building features dark weathered wood throughout. Housed inside are a lounge, a fabulous restaurant, and several upstairs guest rooms boldly decorated with unpeeled log beds, red and black plaids, and faux animal rugs. Number Two has a large wood deck with a view of Tomales Bay through the trees. Its clawfoot tub and original bath fixtures are intact.

An even more fashionable patina is found in the cottages adjacent to the lodge. Manka's Cottage, for instance, is filled with gentlemanly country memorabilia—old fishing tackle boxes, license plates, hunting heirlooms, and an antique globe. In the living room, with its animal rug before the fireplace, tall windows look out to the woods. The kitchenette and bathroom remain much as they were in the twenties, but with luxurious touches added. The bed is piled high with pillows, topping off the romantic atmosphere. Another nearby cabin features a double pedestal tub and outdoor shower.

One mile away is the Chicken Ranch, a two-bedroom guest house (with a "guard pony"), which manager Renata Dorn assured me is their most special accommodation. Renata says prospective guests are not allowed to see it ahead of time. Whenever they want to take a peek, Renata always replies with a Mona Lisa smile, "Just trust me."

Manka's would be a fantastic place to visit for Christmas, when boughs of greenery are draped everywhere. The restaurant, open Thursday through Sunday, is quite renowned in the area. Many of their dishes—the pork chops, quail, and venison sausages, for example—are grilled right in the fireplace while you wait.

MANKA'S INVERNESS LODGE

Telephone: **(415) 669-1034**
Address: **P.O. Box 1110, Inverness 94937**
Rates: **$95 to $265**
Directions: **From Sir Francis Drake Boulevard, three miles north of downtown Inverness, turn left on Argyle Street.**

MONTARA

The Goose & Turrets Bed & Breakfast

Raymond and Emily Hoche-Mong, owners of the Goose & Turrets Bed & Breakfast, like to describe their home this way: "We are a historic, earth-friendly inn catering to readers, nature-lovers, pilots, and enthusiastic eaters." That alone tells you this isn't any ordinary bed and breakfast. It's eccentric, Bohemian, and imperfect, which is why it's not for everyone. But it has character and the most intellectually stimulating innkeepers around.

When you first drive up to this inn, you're greeted by the noisy honking of three mascot geese hidden behind an impossibly tall hedge. Emily says her geese honk differently every time some-one pulls up. She can tell if it's her husband, a guest, the postman, or—God forbid—a dog. With every reservation letter Emily sends out to guests, she encloses a goose feather.

The inn is a 1908 Italianate structure flanked by cannons left over from its days as the Spanish-American War Veterans Country Club. The old, wooden-floored, somewhat musty common area is comfortably cluttered with memorabilia that reflect all the diversified interests of the innkeepers—artwork, photographs, mementos of their many trips, boomerangs, a Spanish-American War flag, games, cookbooks, and a piano, to name a few.

In addition to working hands-on as innkeepers, Raymond and Emily are both active pilots and conservationists. (Emily is a docent naturalist at two local reserves.) One of their guest rooms, the Clipper Room, is wallpapered with every flight chart they've ever used. An old propeller hangs on the wall, and various aeronautical publications are prominently displayed. The canopied bed is swathed in an ethereal blue fabric—an allusion, I suppose, to clouds. Its tiny bathroom across the hall is painted "New Yorker red," with a collage of *New Yorker* magazines papering the walls.

There is also the Lascaux Room, with wall drawings resembling the famous French grotto. Emily is quick to point out the ecologically correct woodstove in this room—it burns gel instead of wood. The remaining bedrooms are more traditional in decor; the Hummingbird Room is the largest and most comfortable. Each bedroom features a towel warmer and—ahem—a goose down feather quilt.

In back, the terraced gardens are lovely, with roses, berry bushes, a fountain, an Appalachian courting swing, and bocce ball. But my eye was drawn to an astounding Monterey cypress hedge surrounding the property. Standing twenty feet high, it's so thick that the gardeners walk on it when they trim it every year.

Breakfast is a four-course affair, with such interesting delicacies as smoked chicken and apple sausage, artichoke-black olive frittata, and crumpets Florentine. Emily claims she can go for twenty-seven days without repeating the same menu. Her afternoon teas might include olallieberry pie, hot mushrooms stuffed with pesto, or tartlets filled with ginger marmalade. You won't go hungry here.

THE GOOSE & TURRETS BED & BREAKFAST

Telephone: **(415) 728-5451; fax (415) 728-0141**
Address: **835 George Street, P.O. Box 937, Montara 94037**
Rates: **$85 to $125, including full breakfast and afternoon tea**
Directions: **From Highway 1 at Montara, turn east on Second Street, right on Main Street, and left on Third, which turns into George Street.**

Point Montara Lighthouse Hostel

There are two lighthouse lodgings along the San Francisco Peninsula, one of which is Point Montara Lighthouse Hostel. Here you stay in bunk rooms adjacent to the lighthouse. As is the case at most hostels, you bring your own linens and clean up after yourself. Bathrooms, fully equipped kitchens, and living rooms are shared. There is also an outdoor hot tub for evening rental. Altogether, it's very similar to Pigeon Point Lighthouse Hostel, farther down the coast. This lighthouse is not as tall or impressive as the one at Pigeon Point—it's sort of short and squat. But this stretch of coastline is great for nature lovers. Between November and April you can watch whales pass by on their annual migration to Baja (bring binoculars and warm clothing). There's also a wonderful marine reserve nearby with one of the best tidepools in the West.

POINT MONTARA LIGHTHOUSE HOSTEL

Telephone: **(415) 728-7177**
Address: **16th Street/Highway 1, Montara 94037**
Rates: **$9 to $11 per person for Hostelling International members; $12 to $14 per person for nonmembers**
Directions: **off Highway 1, between Moss Beach and Montara.**

MOSS BEACH

Seal Cove Inn

Amid the twenty-acre Fitzgerald Marine Reserve on the San Francisco Peninsula, the Seal Cove Inn has a glorious setting. A garden and meadow fill the foreground with color, while a long row of cypress trees guides your eye out to sea. The walk to the cliff's edge is an exhilarating experience. You first pass through a hauntingly beautiful grove of cypress trees. The grove empties out to a bluff high above the ocean. Far below, seals play on the rocks.

Perhaps the most novel aspect about the Seal Cove Inn is that it's owned and designed by a professional travel writer. Well known for her country inn guidebook series, Karen Brown Herbert and her husband, Rick, built the Seal Cove Inn from the ground up and now live there with their two young children. I was curious to see what elements she incorporated into her own inn.

The exterior is built like an English country manor, reflecting, no doubt, some of the inns Karen has covered in Europe. Rick admits that budget constraints put a damper on creating their ultimate fantasy interior. All ten guest rooms, for instance, were constructed with a similar layout, because nowadays it's prohibitively expensive to vary the shape of every single room. But when it came to the little details (far more important anyway), no measure of comfort was spared. Every room has a balcony or patio with view, soft down pillows, thick white towels (two per person) with towel warmers, fluffy terry robes, a wood-burning fireplace with an endless supply of wood, two sinks in the pristine bathroom, a wet bar, and a refrigerator with complimentary bottle of wine and beverages. The luggage racks are in the closets, where they should be, along with sturdy wooden hangers. The television and VCR are hidden in an armoire. Their vast library of free videos comes with popcorn. The showers are strong; the reading and bathroom lights excellent.

Afternoon wine is accompanied by tasty, hot hors d'oeuvres; during turndown, your towels are replaced; in the morning, you'll find the newspaper at your door; at breakfast (you choose the time), the orange juice is freshly squeezed; and, best of all, there is a conspicuous absence of muffins. After eating hundreds of muffins at hundreds of inns, I was delighted to dine without them.

Even without its fantastic setting, the seasoned attention to detail sets this inn apart.

SEAL COVE INN

Telephone:	**(415) 728-4144; fax (415) 728-4116**
Address:	**221 Cypress Avenue, Moss Beach 94038**
Rates:	**$165 to $250 ($15 less single occupancy), including full breakfast in dining room, continental in guest room, and afternoon wine and hors d'oeuvres**
Directions:	**From Highway 1 in Moss Beach, head west on Cypress Avenue (look for the Moss Beach Distillery sign).**

MUIR BEACH

The Pelican Inn

Incurable Anglophiles will find the Pelican Inn a dream come true—as English as any sixteenth-century inn in the Cotswalds. It looks so authentic with its mullioned windows, low doorways, Tudor beams and snug room (private parlor for the guests), you'd never guess it was built as recently as 1979. The wood-paneled pub has all the genuine touches of its British counterparts—low-beamed ceiling covered with foreign bills, dartboards, and a wonderful selection of rich, dark ales and lagers. The only thing it's missing is that distinctive smell of centuries-old stale beer.

The dining room is equally atmospheric with a great brick inglenook fireplace and a priest hold (secret hiding place). The varied dinner menu is accompanied by candlelight and classical music. Breakfast is thoroughly British except, alas, no kippers.

Upstairs, the cozy bedrooms feature heavily draped half-testers (canopy beds) and Oriental rugs. A stone with a hole hangs over the bed, protecting the inn from witches, little folk, and the evil eye—oh, and rickets in case of pregnancy.

This Tudor-style country inn is the creation of Charles Felix, who descends from a long line of British innkeepers. Sir Francis Drake beached his *Pelican* here four hundred years ago to claim California for Queen Elizabeth I. Hence, the Pelican Inn. Just twenty minutes north of San Francisco, the inn is nestled in the fog-shrouded Golden Gate National Recreation Area.

THE PELICAN INN

Telephone: **(415) 383-6000**
Address: **Muir Beach 94965-9729**
Rates: **$143 to $165, including full English breakfast**
Directions: **on Highway 1 in Muir Beach.**

Green Gulch Farm Zen Center

For centuries the monasteries of Japan have offered lodgings to wayfarers from all walks of life. This tradition of unconditional hospitality has been carried on at Green Gulch Farm Zen Center—a Buddhist study center, guest retreat, and organic farm just north of San Francisco.

Everything at Green Gulch is soothingly Zen-like. The peace and quiet is interrupted only by a gong that announces the next meditation period or vegetarian meal. Before entering your Japanese temple-style guest house and airy spare bedroom (with a platform bed or futon), you're expected to remove your shoes.

No one is trying to convert you to Buddhism here. If you're on a personal retreat, you can participate with residents in their activities as much or as little as you like. On Sunday mornings a special Buddhist program is offered to the public: morning meditation instruction, followed by a talk, tea, and lunch. Tea classes in the Urasenke tradition are offered weekly at their traditional Japanese tea house—one of few such structures in America. You can take classes in organic gardening throughout the year.

Anyone is also welcome to hike the trails of the seventy-acre retreat, which makes for a twenty-minute walk down a long, narrow valley of organic gardens to Muir Beach. Walks through the valley and its gardens are particularly memorable.

GREEN GULCH FARM ZEN CENTER

Telephone: **(415) 383-3134; fax (415) 383-3128**
Address: **1601 Shoreline Highway, Sausalito 94965**
Rates: **$55 to $85, single; $90 to $120, double occupancy, including three meals a day**
Directions: **on Highway 1, just south of Muir Beach.**

OAKLAND

Dockside Boat & Bed

This was the first company to start the "boat and breakfast" concept in California in 1989, and the Dockside Boat & Bed is still afloat. Owner Robert Harris and his wife Mollie lease a fleet of luxury yachts, both power and sail, ranging in length from thirty-five to sixty-eight feet. Most of the yachts are moored at Jack London Square in Oakland, but they also have two boats at Pier 39 in San Francisco. Guests spend the night dockside; in the morning, breakfast is delivered to their cabin door. Two of the yachts can be chartered for cruises around the bay as part of a "snooze and cruise" package.

Your choices vary here, and keep in mind these privately owned yachts come and go. My current favorite at their Jack London location is the *Kweilin,* a fifty-four-foot ketch with teak throughout. When I visited, it was docked at the very end of the pier, with an unobstructed view of Alameda Island across the bay. But *Annie's Ark* is their most requested boat in Oakland. It's a smaller vessel—a cozy, thirty-five-foot sailboat with a queen bed in the master stateroom. It's also their lowest-priced selection, and for an extra thirty dollars per person per hour, guests can charter it for sailing.

Of the two boats docked in San Francisco, *Athena* is most popular. This fifty-one-foot modern motor cruiser has three staterooms, two heads with showers, a complete galley, salon, and upper sun deck. The manager of these two vessels has a houseboat-office right on Pier 39.

All boats are equipped with televisions, stereos, coffeemakers, fresh flowers, showers, and heads. Some have microwaves, although elaborate cooking is discouraged. ("If you can nuke it, you can cook it," says Mollie.)

Oakland's Jack London Square is surprisingly pristine, with a cheerful collection of bayfront stores and restaurants. Amtrak (two routes run through Oakland, one going north and south and the other coming from the East via Sacramento) stops right at the square, so don't worry about having to drive. Situated on the inner harbor, you won't have the view that San Francisco offers, but looking across to Alameda Island isn't too shabby.

Mollie says they get all kinds of guests—those who are pondering the purchase of a boat, those who have never been on a boat, and lots of romantic getaways. She and Robert are very flexible about arranging catered dinners, gift baskets, limos, and onboard massages. Robert, a former ad exec, is also a licensed minister. "Whatever it takes to make them happy guests," says Mollie.

DOCKSIDE BOAT & BED

Telephone:	**(800) 4-DOCKSIDE; (510) 444-5858; fax (510) 444-0420**
Address:	**77 Jack London Square, Oakland 94607**
Rates.	**$95 to $275, including continental breakfast**
Directions:	**From I-880 north, exit at Oak Street and head south to Jack London Square; park in the Spaghetti Factory validation lot and look for the Dockside office to your left. From I-880 south, take the Jackson Street exit to Oak Street, then same as above.**

The Claremont Resort

A sprawling white landmark in the Berkeley Hills, the Claremont Resort is easy to spot from miles away. Up close, it's awesome. When I first drove up, the whole structure was glowing pink from the setting sun. Its monumental maze of towers and turrets is almost overwhelming.

The interior is a different kind of pink—old-lady-like and disappointing. And the explosions of ultra-modern art—especially the metal sculpture out front—look abrasively out of place. But minor annoyances aside, stay here for the view alone. From the terrace and many of the rooms, you'll have a fantastic, sweeping panorama of San Francisco Bay, both bridges, and the breathtaking skyline.

If you really want to take advantage of the view, book the Tower Suite, situated in the main tower—the tallest part of the building. Above the bedroom level and inside the very top of the tower is a private sauna and open-air deck with a 360-degree panorama. The Honeymoon Suite also has a special view—one whole wall has been removed and replaced with glass.

Construction of the Claremont began in 1906 and was finished nearly ten years later. The original plans specified that trains would stop inside the lobby, which is easy to imagine from the big arched entry downstairs. Sadly, the concept faded.

In 1936 the Claremont was among very few hotels that lacked a bar, due to a state law that prohibited the sale of alcohol within one mile of a university. It was assumed the Claremont was within the radius of Cal-Berkeley until a female student, who had a great fondness for liquor, began to investigate. She calculated that the hotel was just a few feet outside the prescribed radius. She was given free drinks at the Claremont for the rest of her life.

The Claremont has a full-service spa, and among their more unique body treatments is thetawave—a respiration feedback device that is reputed to deepen breathing levels.

THE CLAREMONT RESORT

Telephone: **(800) 551-7266; (510) 843-3000; fax (510) 848-6208**
Address: **Ashby and Domingo Avenues, Oakland 94623-0363.**
Rates: **$185 to $720; $20 less for single occupancy**
Directions: **From I-80 in Berkeley, exit at Ashby Avenue and head east to the end at Domingo Avenue. You can't miss it.**

PESCADERO

Pigeon Point Lighthouse Hostel

Pigeon Point Lighthouse Hostel is perched on a windy, dramatic cliff fifty miles south of San Francisco. Four three-bedroom houses next to the lighthouse are available to hostellers of all ages. Most bedrooms are male or female bunk rooms, but families and couples can reserve separate quarters. For ten dollars extra, you can have a private room. It's the same setup as Point Montara Lighthouse Hostel, even down to the outdoor hot tub.

The lighthouse itself was built in 1872 after a series of shipwrecks occurred here. (In fact, Pigeon Point is named after the *Carrier Pigeon,* one of the lost ships.) This is the second tallest lighthouse on the West Coast. The lighthouse still operates, but its deafening foghorn was thankfully disconnected in 1972.

PIGEON POINT LIGHTHOUSE HOSTEL

Telephone: **(415) 879-0633 (call between 7:30 and 9:30 A.M. and 5:30 to 9:30 P.M.)**
Address: **210 Pigeon Point Road, Pescadero 94060**
Rates: **$9 to $11 per person for Hostelling International members; $12 to $14 per person for nonmembers**
Directions: **off Highway 1, just south of Pescadero.**

POINT RICHMOND

East Brother Light Station

Poised on an island between San Francisco and San Pablo Bays, East Brother Light Station is the only place in California where you can actually sleep in a lighthouse building. But I'm not sure which is more novel—staying in a lighthouse or overnighting on a little island, within sight of the San Francisco skyline.

Your adventure begins with the bumpy road to San Pablo Harbor, a funky, almost forgotten marina where John Barnett, your innkeeper, picks you up in a small boat. Only ten minutes later, you're approaching East Brother Island, a three-quarter-acre outcropping of rock just big enough to hold the lighthouse, the innkeepers' quarters, a cistern, and the old foghorn station—nothing more. Since there's no convenient access to the island, you climb a vertical ladder from the boat to the pier. (John handles your bags, but pack light.) From here, you're greeted by Lore, John's wife, and two friendly resident dogs, Max and Beacon.

The clapboard lighthouse is not terribly tall—about three stories high—but it's picturesque, with white Victorian trim and a red roof. Constructed in the 1870s, it's the oldest lighthouse still in operation in the San Francisco Bay area. During the foggy months of October through April, the foghorn (which is now solar-powered) blasts every thirty seconds, twenty-four hours a day. Earplugs are provided. But, Lore claims, "In my opinion, the seagulls are more disruptive." I was there in July, when the

At East Brother Light Station, you can actually sleep in a lighthouse.

foghorn was silent and the seagulls, hanging out on nearby West Brother Island, were cawing up a storm. If you lived here all the time, they would drive you nuts.

Within the lighthouse are four guest rooms—two upstairs and two downstairs—with separate parlors and a dining room where everyone eats together. The bedrooms are decorated in unfussy antiques and brass beds. The downstairs rooms share one bath. Because rainwater is the sole water supply, guests aren't allowed to take showers unless they're spending more than one night.

Everyone meets during afternoon wine and hors d'oeuvres, whereupon John takes guests on a tour of the lighthouse and old fog station. He fires up the old-fashioned, diesel-powered foghorn for one deafening "Bee-ooo." At 6:30 P.M., a four-course dinner (complete with wine) is served, often with a seafood entrée. (You should mention any food allergies or dislikes when making your reservation; there is no way off this island for a quick Taco Bell run.) At 9:30 the next morning, everyone gathers in the dining room again for a full breakfast before packing up to shove off at around 11 A.M.

Stays of more than one night aren't overly encouraged here because there isn't a whole lot to do besides read, visit, and bird-watch. (Bring your binoculars.) Except for the occasional passing of a freighter or fishing boat, this part of the bay feels pretty remote.

For ten dollars, by prior arrangement, you can visit for four hours any weekend without staying over, but it takes less than an hour to see the whole place, and day-trippers often grow bored quickly. I'd recommend spending the night. They book several months ahead, so call well in advance.

EAST BROTHER LIGHT STATION

Telephone: **(510) 233-2385**
Reservations: **117 Park Place, Point Richmond 94801**
Rates: **$295, including wine, hors d'oeuvres, dinner, and full breakfast**
Directions: **From I-80, take San Rafael exit to I-580 west to Richmond-San Rafael Bridge; just before the toll plaza, exit at Point Molate; follow signs to San Pablo Yacht Harbor.**

SAN JOSE

LITTLE NOVELTY! Are you the type who gets the munchies at two in the morning? **Hotel De Anza,** an art deco hotel in San Jose, has a "Raid Our Pantry" program. Anytime from 10 P.M. to 5 A.M., guests can help themselves to snacks—cold cuts, sandwiches and salads—in the second floor pantry. For more information, call (800) 843-3700 or (408) 286-1000.

SAN RAFAEL

Panama Hotel

Tucked away on a side street of San Rafael, the Panama Hotel is a funky little tropical oasis operating since 1926. A statue of a pink poodle guards the entry to a palm-filled courtyard cafe (which features blackened foods), and inside, the dining-reception room is packed with campy memorabilia—sombreros, peacock feathers, ballet slippers, pink flamingos, and tacky lamps from the forties and fifties. It's a place more akin to Key West than Marin County.

The guest rooms, in an adjacent building over the cafe, were all occupied when I dropped by, so I can't vouch for them. With names like Ken's Safari Room, Mimi's Bordello, and the Captain's Cabin, they should have something of a theme. I welcome your feedback.

PANAMA HOTEL

Telephone: **(800) 899-3993; (415) 457-3993**
Address: **4 Bayview Street, San Rafael 94901**
Rates: **$45 to $110, including continental breakfast**
Directions: **From US-101, exit at central San Rafael and head west on Third Street; turn left on B Street and continue to the end, where it connects with Bayview Street.**

SARATOGA

Sanborn Park Hostel

Deep in the woods east of Saratoga is Sanborn Park Hostel, a solid old country lodge converted into one of the most tranquil hostels in California. Built entirely of logs in 1908, the lodge was rescued from the bulldozer thanks to the efforts of local volunteers. Now it's available to overnighters of all ages, with spartan dorms and family rooms (bring your own linens and towels), and a fully equipped kitchen where guests cook their own food. Guests also share in chores. The setting is tranquil, with geese honking in the pond nearby and picnic tables nestled in a grove of redwoods.

SANBORN PARK HOSTEL

Telephone: **(408) 741-0166**
Address: **15808 Sanborn Road, Saratoga 95070**
Rates: **$8 for Hostelling International members; $10 for nonmembers**
Directions: **From SR-17, exit at SR-9 to Saratoga; stay on SR-9 and look for Sanborn Road and hostel sign on the left, several miles east of Saratoga.**

SAUSALITO

Casa Madrona Hotel

The steps that lead from downtown Sausalito up to the top of the Casa Madrona Hotel are daunting, to say the least. But the higher you climb, the more delightful it gets. Painted a crisp blue and white—the same colors as the harbor it faces—the hotel is stacked in countless levels up the steep hillside. At the top, where there is a fine restaurant, you'll be rewarded with an outstanding view of the harbor.

With names like Lord Ashley's Lookout and Misia's Lilac and Lace, the guest rooms have been uniquely decorated by art students. Most of the motifs are pretty mild, with a few notable exceptions. Kathmandu, for instance, is filled with lounging cushions, alcoves, mirrors, skylights, and angled ceilings. Artist's Loft comes with an easel, paints, and brushes. Thousand Cranes has a simple Zen-like decor and granite fireplace. In Bridgeway to Hollywood, you have a selection of classic film videos as well as epic movie prints on the walls.

The owners of Casa Madrona also rent out a houseboat at the end of the harbor, one mile north of the hotel. Permanently moored, it features one bedroom, a fireplace, and deck.

By the way—there is an elevator at the hotel, so don't be put off by the steps.

CASA MADRONA HOTEL

Telephone: **(800) 567-9524; (415) 332-0502; fax (415) 332-2537**
Address: **801 Bridgeway, Sausalito 94952**
Rates: **$105 to $245, including continental breakfast**
Directions: **on Bridgeway, in downtown Sausalito.**

WALNUT CREEK

The Mansion at Lakewood

The most unusual thing about the Mansion at Lakewood is its incongruous location in the Walnut Creek suburbs. Originally encompassing two thousand acres, this mansion was the only home in the area back in the 1860s. Although the house itself was expanded, the land was eventually subdivided and pared down to its present three acres. Sharyn and Mike McCoy rescued the rundown mansion from scheduled oblivion and restored it to its former splendor. When the McCoys first moved in, neighbors thought it was haunted. There was no heat, the doors had been kicked in, and only one bathroom had operational plumbing.

Now you'd never recognize the place. A white electronic gate guards the entry to the estate. The gravel driveway leads up to a wide fountain and stops before the polished, white, two-story mansion. Off to one side is an expansive green lawn dotted by white Adirondack chairs.

Inside, the former ballroom has been turned into a vast library, with large windows overlooking the lawns. There's a living and dining room decorated in an elegant country style. Sharyn, who claims she had no previous decorating experience, filled each of the guest rooms with a lavish sense of romance. I especially like Summerhouse, which has a bathroom that's more like a sun porch. Its clawfoot tub is slightly elevated above the pretty, hand-painted floors. In the bedroom, an old vault has been cleverly converted into a walk-in closet. Juliet's Balcony is particularly romantic, with a clawfoot tub surrounded by a little balcony. The Estate Suite also has a wonderful bathroom, with a huge sunken marble Jacuzzi tub and double shower. In the Attic Hideaway, the stairs lead up, then down, into a nook of a bath.

If you get a chance, take a close look at the old American flag that's beveled into the glass over the front door—it has only thirty-four stars.

THE MANSION AT LAKEWOOD

Telephone: **(800) 477-7989; (510) 945-3600**
Address: **1056 Hacienda Drive, Walnut Creek 94598**
Rates: **$135 to $300, including "continental plus" breakfast and afternoon refreshments**
Directions: **From Highway 680 at Walnut Creek, exit and turn right at Ygnacio Valley Road; turn right again at Homestead Avenue and left on Hacienda Drive.**

6 SAN FRANCISCO— THE CITY

Red Victorian Bed & Breakfast

San Francisco boasts a treasure chest of unique lodgings, so I might as well start with the most far-out—the Red Victorian Bed & Breakfast. It's in Haight Ashbury ("the Haight"), painted fire-engine red, and owned by a woman named Sami Sunchild. Need I say more?

Well, okay, a funky, artsy, New Age inn captures the spirit of the Haight. With names like Flower Child, Redwood Forest, and Summer of Love, the guest rooms sound pretty cool.

The inn is all of the above, but most of the bedrooms are a letdown. They look like they haven't been re-touched since the Summer of Love. The rainbows, sixties posters, and intense colors look utterly dated. The Redwood Forest Room, for instance, consists of one of those floor-to-ceiling nature posters that everyone used to hang on their walls to simulate the outdoors. The Cat's Cradle, which formerly offered a live cat named Charlotte to sleep with, is now sadly without Charlotte. (The health department sent her away to a private home.) But the room still has its old cat door, scratching post, and one of the most wonderfully unconventional guest comment books I've seen anywhere.

I prefer the few rooms with international themes, such as the Japanese Tea Garden Room or the Peacock Suite, with its exotic Indian decor and tub next to the bed. The Aquarium Bathroom, a shared bath on the second floor, has a fish tank over the toilet, a sink lined with pebbles, and a trapezoid-shaped shower. And the Playground, with its giant crayons, would be fun for any little flower child.

SAN FRANCISCO—THE CITY

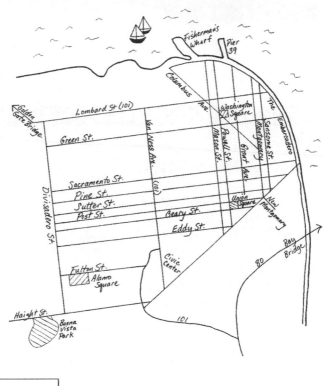

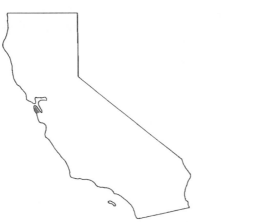

Downstairs is the inn's Peace Center, meant to be a sort of global village for the guests and public. Here, a gallery of meditative art, a mini-meditation room, "life-enhancing" gift shop, and breakfast area—couches, throw pillows, and sheepskin rugs. The pottery (labeled "visual poetry") and artwork ("dreamtime paintings") are all created by Sami Sunchild. She has placed each work of art in a separate niche where you are invited to sit and meditate—similar to a Japanese tokonoma or alcove. This, to me, is the most memorable part of the inn.

If you're a tie-dyed-in-the-wool sixties fan, you'll love this place. But just as the Haight isn't for everyone, neither is the Red Victorian.

RED VICTORIAN BED & BREAKFAST

Telephone: **(415) 864-1978; fax (415) 863-3293**
Address: **1665 Haight Street, San Francisco 94117**
Rates: **$50 to $300, including continental breakfast**
Directions: **on Haight Street at Cole.**

The Spencer House

Also in Haight Ashbury, but on the opposite end of the spectrum from the Red Victorian, is the Spencer House. Once you enter the doors of this fabulous Queen Anne mansion, you leave the hippie-punk, purple-haired neighborhood behind. The Spencer House is the stuff of pure, old-fashioned romance.

How wonderful this inn is—the meticulously restored rooms, the gracious warmth of the owners, Barbara and Jack Chambers, and their splendid collection of one-of-a-kind antiques (many gathered from their travels in the chateau region of France). The stained glass, inlaid wood floors, hand-stenciling, intricate Bradbury and Bradbury wall coverings—they are all of the finest craftsmanship. And the multicourse, candlelit, sterling silver breakfast—it's sublime.

Then there are the beds. They leap from the pages of a fairy tale ("The Princess and the Pea" comes to mind), with the fluffiest down mattresses. I had the best night's sleep ever here. The beds, with their exquisitely carved headboards, are softly lit by original Vaseline globe lamps. Persian rugs, padded walls, old-fashioned vanity tables, and luxurious bathrooms add to the overall romantic atmosphere.

This is a totally impractical inn in which to conduct any business, and it's not a place to visit alone. The Spencer House is a *maison d'amour*—strictly for love.

THE SPENCER HOUSE

Telephone:	**(415) 626-9205; fax (415) 626-9230**
Address:	**1080 Haight Street, San Francisco 94117**
Rates:	**$105 to $165, including full breakfast**
Directions:	**on the corner of Baker and Haight Streets, across from Buena Vista Park.**

LITTLE NOVELTY: Every woman checking into **The Raphael** is presented with a long-stemmed rose. The Raphael is on Geary Street, one block west of Union Square. For more information, call (800) 821-5343 or (415) 986-2000.

The Mansions Hotel

As you climb the steps of these two interconnected Victorian structures and pass the Bufano sculptures in the front yard, a big macaw at the entry hollers, "Hello!" Welcome to the Mansions Hotel.

Along with a flamboyant display of artwork, the Mansions is filled to the brim with the eccentric owner's zany collection of memorabilia. It's kind of like staying at Dali's home—no, make that Fellini. Take the Billiard Room, for example. The pool table is surrounded by a dollhouse-sized Broadway set from Edward Albee's *Tiny Alice* and a hand-painted mural of pigs eating pie. The display cases show off everything from Victorian purses to Jack London's typewriter to an ugly tie collection.

The Music Room is the setting for pre-dinner magic shows and performances by Robert C. Pritikin—proprietor, master of ceremonies, and "America's (self-proclaimed) foremost classical saw player." His saw selections are accompanied by the invisible fingers of resident ghost Claudia Chambers. (She is also the scapegoat for any problems that beset the hotel.) The show, included with dinner, is best seen on Fridays or Saturdays; on weekdays, they scale it down. After the show, guests move on to the dining room, which purportedly contains the world's longest continual stained-glass scene. If you're so inclined to take home an album of Pritikin's saw music, or one of Pritikin's books, or a bottle of Pig's Leap wine, all these wacky gift items are available for sale.

The guest quarters vary in size from the tiny Tom Thumb Room to the lavish Josephine Suite. The walls of each guest room are painted with murals depicting the historic personage to whom each room is dedicated. Contributing to the hotel's "porkabilia" are pig paintings in every room.

Although none of this seems to make any sense whatsoever, Pritikin, a former ad man, knows exactly what he's doing. He discovered early on that the more deliberately outlandish he made his inn, the more attention and business it would draw. His gimmickry has worked—his guest list includes everyone from Barbra Streisand to Robin Williams to the late Andrei Sakharov.

THE MANSIONS HOTEL

Telephone: **(415) 929-9444**
Address: **2220 Sacramento Street, San Francisco 94115**
Rates: **$129 to $350, including full breakfast**
Directions: **on Sacramento Street, between Laguna and Buchanan Streets.**

The Phoenix

The Phoenix claims to be the only San Francisco hotel that caters to rock and roll groups, meaning receptionists here are accustomed to late-night check-ins and noise. (Black Sabbath was staying here when I visited.) But the hotel is also popular with the entertainment crowd because it's so un-San Francisco-like. Painted turquoise and coral, the two-story motel surrounds a swimming pool with palm trees, and its rooms are decorated in tropical rattan. Their campy Caribbean restaurant, Miss Pearl's Jam House, features reggae music. All of this, smack in downtown San Francisco.

But what makes the Phoenix really hip are its offbeat little touches. When you check in, you get a free Phoenix tattoo sticker; all of the rooms come with xylophones to play; and an in-house TV channel features films made exclusively in San Francisco. In addition to the local artwork in every room, colorful sculptures have been placed around the swimming pool. Even the bottom of the pool (copyrighted by the artist) is painted in blue swirls.

It's nearly impossible to find any hotel in the city that offers so much personality, free parking, and continental breakfast for only eighty-nine dollars a night.

THE PHOENIX

Telephone:	**(800) CITY-INN; (415) 776-1380; fax (415) 885-3109**
Address:	**601 Eddy Street, San Francisco 94109**
Rates:	**$89, including continental breakfast**
Directions:	**on Eddy and Larkin Streets, two blocks east of Van Ness Avenue.**

Hotel Triton

Also hip but on a more upscale level is the Hotel Triton. I love the Triton because it's full of playfulness and cutting-edge surprises, yet it's run with the same smooth efficiency and sophistication found at any fine hotel.

The whimsy begins with the bellman outside the front door. Outfitted like a cast member of the *Cirque du Soleil,* he might be wearing an asymmetrical costume and bowler hat, or shoes with curlicue toes. Everything in the lobby is asymmetrical, too, from the wavy gold columns, to the undulating chairs, to the wiggly, loopy lamps. Murals of mythological elements (such as human figures and sea life), hand painted in soft shades of blue, green, and violet, flow dreamily on the walls. A royal blue carpet dotted with gold stars adds even more intense color to the room. The reception staff, in contrast, are dressed in chic black or white. You've passed through the looking glass to a very hip Wonderland.

This theme carries on to the guest rooms, which range from mildly novel to wild. The walls are hand painted in soft, oversize checks or diamonds, while many of the furnishings and pillows feature bold stripes or geometric patterns. Above every bed is a golden star. The light fixtures might shoot out of the ceiling like bolts of lightning or curve around in circles. The artwork, vanity counters, armoires—everything is startlingly original. Even the usual Do Not Disturb sign reads Leave Me Alone!

Everything in Hotel Triton's lobby is asymmetrical.

The Triton has invited an eclectic handful of celebrity designers to the scene, granting each one full license to do his or her own thing to one guest room. There's the J. Garcia Suite, filled with prismatic fabrics drawn from the artwork of the late Grateful Dead member. (What an irony that this anti-establishment figure sold more than a million neckties.) His paintings and signature are hung on the walls. Even the shower curtain is a Jerry Garcia design.

Another suite was created by Suzan Briganti, the handbag designer. Done in rich black and cream, this suite focuses on romance. The duvet cover fabric is printed with love letters, and actual love letters are framed on the walls. The bathroom mirror is outlined with silk roses, while the folding screen features various mementos from love affairs. At check-in, guests receive a love letter from Briganti. There's also a rather garish safari-style suite designed by Joe Boxer of underwear fame, plus a Wyland-inspired suite of underwater themes, complete with an aquarium of tropical fish.

The Triton also has a series of Eco-Rooms, designed with environmental sensitivity in mind. Here you will find biodegradable soap and shampoo, energy-efficient lighting and temperature control, water-saving shower and toilet devices, an air and water-filtering system, and all natural cotton linens. The rooms are cleaned with biodegradable products, as well. The hotel hopes to transform all of the guest rooms into Eco-Rooms eventually. In every room, you can opt to keep the same towels as long as you wish to save on energy.

Naturally, the Triton draws a lot of trendy, artsy guests and a quirky collection of celebrities—among them Lily Tomlin, the Psychedelic Furs, and David Cassidy. When the evening wine is served in the lobby, it's a great time for people-watching. The guests are as interesting as the hotel.

Hotel Triton is a perfect location if you want to be downtown. The gates of Chinatown are right outside, and Union Square is two blocks away. After staying here, the more traditional downtown hotels seem quite ho-hum.

HOTEL TRITON

Telephone: **(800) 433-6611; (415) 394-0500; fax (415) 394-0555**
Address: **342 Grant Avenue, San Francisco 94108**
Rates: **$105 to $285, including afternoon wine and morning coffee; $20 for valet parking**
Directions: **two blocks northeast of Union Square, at Bush Street and Grant Avenue.**

LITTLE NOVELTY: At the **Commodore International Hotel** in San Francisco, you're greeted by a wheel of fortune at check-in, and every guest wins something, such as drinks at the Tonga Room or a free walking tour. For more information, contact the Commodore International Hotel at (800) 338-6848 or (415) 923-6800.

Mandarin Oriental San Francisco

For the most stupendous view of San Francisco, try a Mandarin Room at the Mandarin Oriental San Francisco. Occupying the top eleven floors of the city's third tallest building, the rooms have a spectacular panorama of the bay and skyline. And the Mandarin Rooms (there are only two on each floor) have marble soaking tubs set against full-length picture windows. Imagine taking a bubble bath from the forty-eighth floor at eye level with the top of the TransAmerica building only a few blocks away. If you request a Mandarin Room with Golden Gate view, you get a 180-degree vista of both bridges. If you have a fear of heights, forget it.

Guests can bathe in splendor at the Mandarin Oriental San Francisco.

The Mandarin offers other unusual amenities. Upon arrival, guests are presented with jasmine tea and silk slippers. Fresh-baked cookies arrive with turndown service. And since most of their weekday guests are American business travelers, every room is equipped with three phones and two lines.

MANDARIN ORIENTAL SAN FRANCISCO

Telephone: **(415) 885-0999; fax (415) 433-0289**
Address: **222 Sansome Street, San Francisco 94104-2792**
Rates: **$275 to $1,295 ($395 for a Mandarin Room)**
Directions: **in the Financial District, between California and Pine Streets.**

Miyako Hotel

The Miyako has six traditional Japanese-style guest rooms that are quite exotic. A gate slides open to the sitting area, which features a rock garden and walls of shoji screens. The futon bed is raised on a platform of tatami mats. In addition to the shower, there's a Japanese soaking tub in the bathroom. An alcove, or tokonoma, is used to display Japanese art.

If you really want to immerse yourself in the culture, Japantown is right outside the door. After a day of exploring, you can enjoy a shiatsu massage right in your room.

MIYAKO HOTEL

Telephone: **(800) 533-4567; (415) 922-3200; fax (415) 921-0417**
Address: **1625 Post Street, San Francisco 94115**
Rates: **$139 to $299 ($279 for a Japanese Suite), including American breakfast**
Directions: **on Post Street, between Laguna and Webster Streets.**

LITTLE NOVELTY: Every room at the healthful **Nob Hill Lambourne** is stocked with exercise equipment and a natural remedy bar: echinacea for colds, chamomile for insomnia, Siberian ginseng for increased vitality, and healthful snacks. At turndown, they place a beta-carotene tablet and philosophical goodnight thought on your pillow instead of the usual chocolate. For more information, call (800) BRITINN or (415) 433-2287.

The Archbishop's Mansion

Among all the wonderful inns of San Francisco, the Archbishop's Mansion is one of the most luxurious. Built for the archbishop of San Francisco in 1904, it's as grand as a palace, with high ceilings, chandeliers, and resplendent belle époque furnishings. Positioned under a sixteen-foot stained-glass dome is a three-story carved mahogany staircase leading up to the guest quarters.

The bedrooms, all named after romantic operas, are truly resplendent with Oriental rugs, rich fabrics, and warm wood trim. The Don Giovanni Suite boasts two fireplaces, a shower with seven heads, and an ornately carved four-poster bed imported from a French castle. In the Gypsy Baron Suite (once the archbishop's chapel), a double tub has been built into the altar where baptisms were once performed. But my favorite, and the most requested, is the Carmen Suite. Its bathroom is decorated like an intimate salon, with a clawfoot tub placed directly before the carved wood fireplace. All bathrooms offer honor baskets of aromatherapy toiletries. And if your quixotic nature needs any further nudging, all of the inn's video selections are romantic movies.

In the parlor the hand-painted ceiling has been detailed just like a nineteenth-century Aubusson carpet. A 1904 Bechstein grand piano, once owned by Nöel Coward, is played during the afternoon wine hour. Those who are inspired to enjoy a night at the opera six blocks away can arrange for a limousine ride to the front steps.

If you can tear yourself away from your tub for a few moments, hike up to the top of the grassy hill on Alamo Square across from the inn. From here, you'll recognize that much-photographed San Francisco skyline scene, with its row of colorful Victorian homes in the foreground and the downtown skyscrapers in the background.

THE ARCHBISHOP'S MANSION

Telephone:	**(800) 543-5820; (415) 563-7872; fax (415) 885-3193**
Address:	**1000 Fulton Street, San Francisco 94117**
Rates:	**$129 to $385, including continental breakfast and afternoon wine**
Directions:	**on the northeast corner of Alamo Square at Steiner and Fulton Streets.**

The Sherman House

Although it ranks up there with the Archbishop's Mansion in luxury, the Sherman House's modest foyer gives no hint of the posh treats that lie beyond. But climb up the stairs to the next landing and suddenly a fabulous, ballroom-sized music room opens up before you. Built in 1901 by the great patron of the arts, Leander Sherman, this grand, skylit room was added to the mansion to accommodate impromptu concerts. Ignacy Paderewski was once a frequent guest. A grand piano still sits in the salon, as well as a chateau-style cage of singing finches.

Many of the guest rooms have canopied beds that are romantically closed up at turndown. Among the most unique rooms are the Biedermeier Suite, lushly appointed in tapestry and silk, and the Sherman Suite, with its unobstructed bay view. Also intriguing is the Paderewski Suite, formerly the billiards room. It's furnished in the Jacobean period, with dark wood wainscoting, wood-beamed ceiling, and two fireplaces. At $625 a night, however, you'll pay dearly for your 1600s ambiance.

The dining room is exclusively for the guests' use, and each evening your personalized menu can be printed with a special message upon request. For a really intimate experience, you can have dinner served in your room. This is the good life.

THE SHERMAN HOUSE

Telephone: **(800) 424-5777; (415) 563-3600; fax (415) 563-1882**
Address: **2160 Green Street, San Francisco 94123**
Rates: **$190 to $825**
Directions: **on Green Street, between Webster and Fillmore Streets.**

LITTLE NOVELTY: If you stay in a room facing the park at **Washington Square Inn**, you will awaken in the morning to find hundreds of people practicing t'ai chi before the cathedral. Situated on the border of the Italian district and Chinatown, this bed and breakfast has a great location—especially for lovers of good food. For more information, call the Washington Square Inn at (415) 981-4220.

The Westin St. Francis

No matter where you stay in San Francisco, have a glass of champagne or afternoon tea in the Compass Rose Room of the Westin St. Francis on Union Square. Designed by Joszi Meskan, it's one of the most beautifully appointed bars in San Francisco. Under the high, ornate ceilings and fluted columns, Oriental antiques, plush love seats, and art nouveau chairs are grouped randomly together in intimate little circles. Among the many museum-quality curios in this exquisite room are a Bible screen from sixteenth-century China, Korean cloisonné vases, a Moroccan table inlaid with mother-of-pearl, and eighteenth-century English settees from Brighton Pavilion. Everything blends beautifully into a darkly exotic flavor I never tire looking at.

THE WESTIN ST. FRANCIS

Telephone: **(800) 228-3000 or (415) 397-7000; fax (415) 774-0124**
Address: **335 Powell Street, San Francisco 94102**
Rates: **$180 to $275; $30 less for single occupancy**
Directions: **on Union Square.**

Sheraton Palace Hotel

The most dazzling dining room in San Francisco is in the Sheraton Palace Hotel. With its lofty, domed ceiling of stained glass (eighty thousand panes, to be exact), the Garden Court is reminiscent of the magnificent Crystal Palace in nineteenth-century England. Marble columns and huge chandeliers add to its nineteenth-century splendor. While enjoying afternoon tea or Sunday brunch, beware of a neckache from looking up.

SHERATON PALACE HOTEL

Telephone: **(800) 325-3535; (415) 392-8600; fax (415) 543-0671**
Address: **2 New Montgomery Street, San Francisco 94105**
Rates: **$235 to $2,600, single; $255 to $2,600, double**
Directions: **on New Montgomery Street, three blocks east of Union Square.**

Fairmont Hotel

The prize for grandest classic lobby in San Francisco goes to the Fairmont Hotel—a veritable European palace with its marble columns, chandeliers, ruby velvet sofas, and gold-leaf trim. It's no wonder more than twenty movies have been filmed here—this is classic old San Francisco opulence.

For a mere six thousand dollars, you can spend a night in the Penthouse Suite, which occupies the entire eighth floor. This eight-room suite includes an immense drawing room with grand piano; a dining room for up to fifty guests; a two-story circular library with the celestial constellation in gold on its domed ceiling; a billiards room with Persian-tiled walls and stained-glass skylight; three bedrooms and four baths with twenty-four-karat gold fixtures; a full kitchen and secret passageway. Four of the fireplaces are inlaid with lapis lazuli, marble, and woods. The 100 percent goose feathers in the pillows are imported from Ireland. A butler and maid are available around the clock.

For the rest of us peons who occupy the lower floors, the Fairmont offers complimentary chicken soup to anyone who has taken cold.

FAIRMONT HOTEL

Telephone: **(800) 527-4727; (415) 772-5000; fax (415) 772-5086**
Address: **950 Mason Street, San Francisco 94108-2098**
Rates: **$209 to $6,000; $20 less for single occupancy**
Directions: **on Nob Hill, between Sacramento and California Streets.**

Hyatt Regency San Francisco

Among contemporary lobbies, no hotel matches the Hyatt Regency San Francisco. Designed by John Portman (who also did the Bonaventure in L.A.), its phenomenal atrium is a boggling architectural masterpiece—a seven-sided pyramid with twenty stories of hanging gardens. A huge aluminum sculpture rises out of a reflecting pond four stories up into the atrium. You must go down to the Embarcadero just to see this lobby.

HYATT REGENCY SAN FRANCISCO

Telephone: **(415) 788-1234; fax (415) 398-2567**
Address: **5 Embarcadero Center, San Francisco 94111**
Rates: **$149 to $230**
Directions: **in the Embarcadero, at the foot of California Street.**

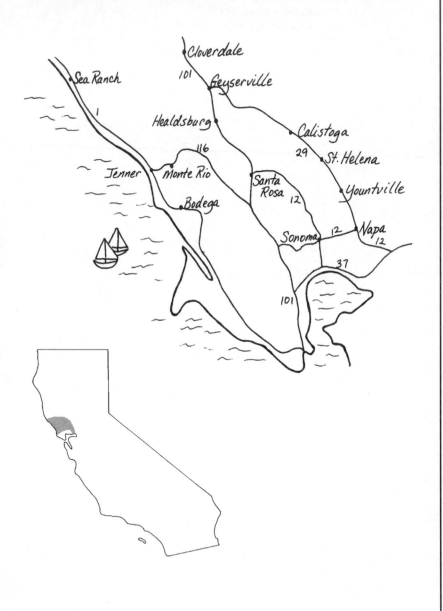

NAPA AND SONOMA COUNTIES

Sea Ranch

1

Cloverdale

101

Geyserville

Healdsburg

116

Jenner

Monte Rio

Bodega

Santa Rosa

12

Calistoga

29

St. Helena

Yountville

Sonoma

12

Napa

12

37

101

BODEGA

Bodega Estero Bed & Breakfast

If you ever wondered what the inside of a geodetic dome looks like, find out at Bodega Estero Bed & Breakfast. Set in the coastal hills south of Bodega, it's the only geodetic-domed bed and breakfast in California. All of the ceilings are uniquely angled. The airy living room has two-story, open-beamed ceilings and multiple windows.

Another unusual aspect of the inn has nothing to do with its shape: Hosts Michael and Edgar raise a llama, angora goats, and several types of sheep whose fleeces are sheared and spun into yarn. The innkeepers weave and knit the wool themselves, as the miscellaneous looms and spinning wheels in the living room attest.

BODEGA ESTERO BED & BREAKFAST

Telephone: **(800) 422-6321; (707) 876-3300**
Address: **17699 Highway 1, P.O. Box 362, Bodega 94922**
Rates: **$75 to $100, including afternoon wine and continental breakfast**
Directions: **on Highway 1, five miles south of Bodega.**

CALISTOGA

Indian Springs

Although Calistoga is in the heart of the wine country, most people come to this town for the mud baths and hot springs. The main street is lined with mostly homely motels offering spa and mud bath packages. Indian Springs is one of the few spas with character.

Open since 1865, Indian Springs is one of California's oldest continuously operating spas. The Olympic-sized, Mission-style pool was built in 1913, but its blue-green waters look so refreshing, it could be brand new. Naturally heated by geysers, the pool ranges from 92 to 101 degrees.

The mud bathhouse is a classic early California building—white adobe with red-tile roof—also built in 1913. A mud bath here consists of four stages. First, you lie in a tub of pure, warm volcanic ash mixed with hot, sterilizing mineral water. The heat induces perspiration, which helps cleanse your system. After ten minutes or so, you shower off and soak in a Victorian tub of mineral water. If you wish, you can continue with a geyser water steam bath. Finally, you're swaddled in blankets to rest and cool down. To extend the experience another hour, you can have a massage. Many people find the mud bath relaxing enough by itself.

Accommodations consist of several no-frills forties cottages with plank floors and gas fireplaces. Nothing fancy, but they're better than most of the boring motels in the area.

Adjacent to Indian Springs is a gliderport which offers special rates on glider rides to Indian Springs guests.

INDIAN SPRINGS

Telephone:	**(707) 942-4913**
Address:	**1712 Lincoln Avenue, Calistoga 94515**
Rates:	**$105 to $160; $50 for a mud bath treatment**
Directions:	**in Calistoga, on SR-29; open to day visitors.**

Mount View Hotel

Even though some people are squeamish about immersing themselves in a thick mud bath, most are at least curious. For these, I suggest the Mount View Hotel in downtown Calistoga. Here they offer a lighter version of the traditional mud bath: Fango mud. A mixture of pine oil, salicyl (the base of aspirin), and volcanic ash is dissolved in water, and jets are turned on to keep the water circulating. The mud is quite thin—almost the consistency of water—

LITTLE NOVELTY: If you like angels, book the Angel Room at **The Pink Mansion** in Calistoga. At least twenty-five cherubs and angels are scattered throughout the bedroom of this friendly pink Victorian. For more information, call the Pink Mansion at (800) 238-PINK or (707) 942-0558.

and fragrant, too. Each treatment is conducted in a private room that can accommodate an individual or a couple. You can also opt for a mud wrap, where your entire body is painted with a mixture of Dead Sea mud, honey, and glycerin, then wrapped in warm blankets.

The rooms of this historic hotel are more upscale than the other lodgings of Calistoga, and two are furnished in Hollywood art deco decor. Ask for the Jean Harlow Room or Carole Lombard Room.

MOUNT VIEW HOTEL

Telephone:	**(707) 942-6877; fax (707) 942-6904**
Address:	**1457 Lincoln Avenue, Calistoga 94515**
Rates:	**$85 to $190**
Directions:	**in downtown Calistoga, on SR-29.**

CLOVERDALE

LITTLE NOVELTY: At **Ye Olde Shelford House** in Cloverdale, you can tour the wineries of northern Sonoma County in the innkeepers' 1929 Ford Model A. Upon return, you'll enjoy a picnic lunch in their wine-barrel gazebo. For more information, call (800) 833-6479 or (707) 894-5956.

GEYSERVILLE

Isis Oasis

Here is a retreat that pretty much defies categorization. Its brochure describes "a gathering place for groups and individuals seeking an extraordinary environment for mind, body, and spirit."

The Meditation Temple at Isis Oasis greets visitors seeking rest for mind, body, and spirit.

The first thing you encounter when you drive up is an obelisk and Egyptian meditation temple. And this is only the beginning.

Scattered over ten acres of rural hillsides are an eclectic variety of accommodations. If you want to go the comfortable route, then stay in a lodge room, a suite in a Victorian house, a cottage for two, or a narrow, two-story tower. But if you prefer a walk on the wild side, there are more rustic lodgings— different-sized yurts, a tepee, a minipyramid, and even a room built into a wine barrel with a shared bathhouse.

Although they might be hot and stuffy during the warm Geyserville summers, yurts are otherwise quite nice inside . . . for yurts, that is. Some have stained-glass doors or crystals at the entry and beds covered with Indian or simulated leopard-skin spreads. The giant yurt, which comfortably holds seven mattresses on the floor, has a little vanity table with a mirror and wing-back wicker chair. The tepee is more rustic with a dirt floor and lots of spider webs up in the apex, although it does have a real bed. The wooden minipyramid, painted white, blue, and violet, is about the size of a two-person tent.

My personal favorite among the rustic novelties was the wine-barrel room. Nestled in a gully under the trees, this converted wine barrel has a skylight and little wood deck. It's nothing fancy—just big enough to hold a wicker bed and antique armoire. But it looks—ahem—like a barrel of fun.

Egypt is a major theme here. (Isis was the Egyptian goddess of nature.) Exotic reminders of Egypt are in every detail, from the ankh stained-glass windows, to the Egyptian artwork, to the Egyptian shower curtains. Little mirrors and peacock feathers are arranged in most of the rooms. The whole place has a hushed, meditative atmosphere. Only the occasional cry of a peacock breaks the silence.

In the aviaries and private lodgings are a collection of exotic birds, llamas, and goats, plus a few large felines (considered sacred animals in Egypt): ocelots, servals, bobcats, and even a Bengal tiger.

Elsewhere on the grounds are a swimming pool and sauna (also built into a wine barrel), a dining pavilion, and theater where retreat groups gather. During a mild season, this would make a pleasant retreat for quiet meditation. And just in case there's not enough exotica to hold your attention, the staff also provides massage therapy, facials, yoga sessions, and tarot or past-life readings.

ISIS OASIS

Telephone: **(707) 857-3524**
Address: **20889 Geyserville Avenue, Geyserville 95411**
Rates: **$45 to $200, including breakfast in some rooms; discounts available for two-night stays; pets welcome in some accommodations**
Directions: **From US-101, exit at Geyserville and follow the signs to Geyserville Avenue. Isis Oasis is on the south end of town.**

HEALDSBURG

Grape Leaf Inn

This Victorian house is painted a delicious violet and periwinkle, with little stars dotting the white trim. The sign by the door says, "One very nice person and one old grouch live here." A comfy, funky place, the Grape Leaf Inn has one rather unique room among its guest quarters. Nestled up among the dormers, the Chardonnay Suite features oddly angled ceilings highlighted by four skylight windows. The wall of each cedar-lined dormer is punctuated by a stained-glass window of purple and blue. In the bathroom is a whirlpool tub-shower for two. The Cabernet Sauvignon Room also has a nice whirlpool tub under a skylit roof.

On most Saturday evenings, the innkeepers invite a local Sonoma County vintner to present his or her wines to guests.

GRAPE LEAF INN

Telephone: **(707) 433-8140**
Address: **539 Johnson Street, Healdsburg 95448**
Rates: **$90 to $145, including full breakfast and afternoon wine and cheese**
Directions: **From US-101, exit at Mill Street and head east; turn left on Healdsburg Avenue, right on Grant Street, and right on Johnson Street.**

Belle de Jour Inn

What better way to cool off from a long day of Sonoma County wine tasting than a dip in a wine vat? At the Belle de Jour Inn, the little pool is built out of an old twenty-five-thousand-gallon wine vat. Picturesquely set on the hillside, it overlooks the main house and white guest cottages. If further soaking is in order, three of the four rooms feature whirlpool tubs. The Morning Hill Room has its own steam shower.

For an additional charge, innkeepers Tom and Brenda Hearn will take guests on chauffeured back roads and winery tours in their 1925 Star Tourer.

BELLE DE JOUR INN

Telephone: **(707) 431-9777; fax (707) 431-7412**
Address: **16276 Healdsburg Avenue, Healdsburg 95448**
Rates: **$125 to $185, including full breakfast**
Directions: **From US-101, exit at Dry Creek Road and head east; turn left on Healdsburg Avenue and proceed one mile; inn is on right, across from Simi Winery.**

JENNER

Timber Cove Inn

Poised on a rocky promontory above a rugged stretch of coastline, Timber Cove Inn is distinguished by a striking obelisk rising seventy-two feet from the edge of the cliff. Called the *Expanding Universe,* it is Beniamino Bufano's largest work.

The obelisk at Timber Cove Inn rises seventy-two feet skyward.

The rugged redwood lodge consists of a massive lobby, bar, and walk-in stone fireplace. Outside the lobby, a Japanese pool emerges from under the building. In the center of the pool is a casting of a torso, also by Bufano.

Aside from a few pieces of driftwood and prints by Ansel Adams, the guest rooms are almost completely lacking in decor. I don't mean the decor is bad—there simply is no decor. The five-room honeymoon suite, for example, is big and has a spectacular view from the balcony, but that's about it. The apparent intent was to remove all distractions so the eye would be drawn to the scene outside. I admired their philosophy but found the interiors almost depressingly spartan. How about some sprays of wildflowers, at least?

This is a contemplative, Zen-like sort of place. The rooms have no phones or televisions. If you're happy just perusing nature, hiking, and watching the surf crash on the rocks, then Timber Cove Inn might be just right. If not, at least stop here and pick up a cocktail napkin from the bar—it explains the story behind the obelisk.

TIMBER COVE INN

Telephone:	**(707) 847-3231; fax (707) 847-3704**
Address:	**21780 North Coast Highway 1, Jenner 95450**
Rates:	**$78 to $350**
Directions:	**on Highway 1, fifteen miles north of Jenner.**

MONTE RIO

Huckleberry Springs Country Inn

One of the guest cottages at Huckleberry Springs Country Inn is a converted cherry barrel with original staves still intact. Sixteen feet in diameter, it has enough room for a wood-burning stove.

This Russian River mountaintop retreat is quite secluded, with a beautiful approach up a winding dirt road. Only four guest cottages are spread throughout the sixty acres, ensuring maximum privacy. They are delightfully unfrilly, with contemporary decor, simple lines, platform beds, and modern luxuries such as VCRs, hair dryers, and stereos. A new massage building has been added to the Japanese-style spa on a hillside above the airy main lodge. (Call at least one week in advance for a massage.) On Saturday and Wednesday evenings, owner Suzanne Greene will, upon request, prepare a four-course meal in the lodge.

HUCKLEBERRY SPRINGS COUNTRY INN

Telephone:	(800) 822-2683; (707) 865-2683
Address:	P.O. Box 400, Monte Rio 95462
Rates:	$125, single; $145, double, including breakfast
Directions:	From Monte Rio, on the south side of the Russian River, take Main Street south to Tyrone Road; turn right, and then right again on Old Beedle Road, which becomes a dirt road. Visits by appointment only.

NAPA

Churchill Manor

Innkeepers Joanna Guidotti and Brian Jensen host nearly fifty weddings a year at Churchill Manor. No wonder. Built in 1889, this pink and white Colonial Revival mansion is encircled by a wide verandah, white columns, and a luxuriant lawn outlined by picture-perfect roses. The interior encompasses ten thousand square feet of elbow room. At the entry there's an elegant salon-reception area filled with Oriental carpets, leather sofas, redwood paneling, and burgundy velvet drapes. There's also a music room with chandelier and grand piano, as well as a dining room, game room, and, finally, the sun room, its floors laid with sixty thousand original tiles. Upstairs are ten antique bedrooms. This place is made for weddings.

Churchill Manor is not just an ideal wedding site, but also the most impressive place to stay in the town of Napa. It's elegant without being a look-but-don't-touch kind of place. A tirelessly energetic couple, Joanna and Brian set an informal tone that makes everyone feel comfortable. During the winter, they host mystery weekends with full plays and gourmet dinners. When I was there, Joanna was toying with the idea of starting some special "baby weekends," when couples could bring their infants to the inn.

I must again mention the roses—the most beautiful roses I've seen at any inn. Among the more novel names of the fifty-plus varieties are Helmut Schmidt, Lucille Ball, Ingrid Bergman, and— Joanna's favorite—Abracadabra. During my visit, Joanna was preparing for a full-scale wedding the next day. Wedding party guests were busily coming and going, Joanna's baby was crawling about, and Joanna still took time to worry about her beloved roses. "My Barbara Bush hasn't been doing too well," she bemoaned.

CHURCHILL MANOR

Telephone:	**(707) 253-7733; fax (707) 253-8836**
Address:	**485 Brown Street, Napa 94559**
Rates:	**$75 to $145, including full breakfast and afternoon wine**
Directions:	**From SR-29, exit at First Street/Central Napa. Follow "downtown Napa" signs onto Second Street; turn right on Jefferson Street, left on Oak Street, and proceed seven blocks to Brown Street.**

ST. HELENA

The Ink House

Distinguished by its central, fifty-foot belvedere, the Ink House resembles an inkwell stopper. At the top of the observatory is a glass-walled parlor where guests can enjoy a 360-degree view of the Napa Valley vineyards. If you're lucky, you might catch sight of a hot air balloon floating by. The little observatory is filled with white wicker furnishings, stained-glass windows, and plants.

The Italianate Victorian inn has a tastefully appointed interior, enhanced by the fresh fragrance of potpourri. Although most of the bedrooms are traditional in decor, the Hawaii Room features artwork by contemporary artists from Hawaii—a reminder of the late 1800s when Hawaii's king and consort paid frequent visits to their friend and Napa Valley resident, Robert Louis Stevenson.

THE INK HOUSE

Telephone: **(800) 553-4343; (707) 963-3890**
Address: **1575 St. Helena Highway, St. Helena 94574**
Rates: **$125 to $145, including continental breakfast**
Directions: **on SR-29 and Whitehall Lane, between Rutherford and St. Helena.**

Meadowood

From the floor of the Napa Valley, you wind slowly up a wooded hill into the 250-acre resort of Meadowood. Meandering through the stately grounds are a health spa, lodge, restaurant, conference center, guest buildings, croquet lawns, tennis courts, golf course, and swimming pool. Meadowood is sprawling, yet it has a very private, secluded feel because of all the trees (a happy result of its former days as a Christmas-tree farm).

Aside from its beautiful setting, Meadowood is known for two unique features—its wine school and world-class croquet. The Meadowood Wine School offers wine and food courses for both experts and beginners. Among their classes: Spirited Wine Tasting Games, Winery Tours, Vineyard Picnics, and Winemaker's Dinners. With 273 Napa Valley wines on hand, you learn about the newest releases as well as Napa classics. Make no mistake—wine is a big pastime at Meadowood. In fact, sipping wine is considered part of your workout at the health spa.

Croquet is also a big focus at Meadowood. It has two full-sized, world-class courts, or lawns, and the resident pro happens to be captain of the Olympic croquet team. The manicured setting looks like something out of a Merchant-Ivory film. It doesn't matter if you're a beginner or a pro—this game makes everyone look good. And as those at Meadowood like to say, "In no other game can you sip tea or champagne, smoke a Havana, and sit in a lounge chair—between shots."

MEADOWOOD

Telephone: **(800) 458-8080; (707) 963-3646; fax (707) 963-3532**
Address: **900 Meadowood Lane, St. Helena 94574**
Rates: **$280–$1,875**
Directions: **From SR-29, head east on Zinfandel Lane, north of Rutherford; turn left on Silverado Trail, right on Howell Mountain Road, then left on Meadowood Lane.**

Next stop, Melitta Station, a turn-of-the-century railroad depot.

Melitta Station Inn

Just east of Santa Rosa is a converted, turn-of-the-century railroad depot known as Melitta Station Inn. Although the interior—filled with cute bed and breakfast bunnies and patchwork quilts—is unrecognizable from its former days, the long, red clapboard building still looks very much like a depot on the outside. It sits in a quiet, tree-lined residential neighborhood.

MELITTA STATION INN

Telephone:	**(707) 538-7712**
Address:	**5850 Melitta Road, Santa Rosa 95409**
Rates:	**$80 to $90, including full breakfast and afternoon wine**
Directions:	**From US-101 at Santa Rosa, head east on SR-12; turn right on Melitta Road and proceed for one mile.**

SEA RANCH

The Sea Ranch Lodge

Sea Ranch is well known for its collection of environmentally unobtrusive homes built along the windswept coast of Northern California back in the seventies. Constructed of weathered wood, they're all slightly different. Since its early days, the experimental complex has turned into a substantial community of a thousand homes, with its own post office and chapel (which, incidentally, is well worth seeing).

You don't have to own one of the homes to spend the night here. Just beyond the post office is the Sea Ranch Lodge, built of weathered wood and available to overnight guests. The rooms are paneled in wood, with patchwork quilts and unframed nature photographs on the walls. Most have dramatic ocean views, fireplaces, and hot tubs, although there are no phones or TVs.

The main source of activity at the Sea Ranch is the Scottish-links-style golf course, and the lodge offers a variety of golf packages. Although it has grown up since the seventies, the Sea Ranch is still an eye-catching development.

THE SEA RANCH LODGE

Telephone: **(800) SEA-RANCH; (707) 785-2371**
Address: **P.O. Box 44, Sea Ranch 95497**
Rates: **$125 to $180**
Directions: **off Highway 1, near the south end of Sea Ranch.**

SONOMA

Sonoma Chalet

Here's a place with a funky forties feel that adds tremendously to its charm. The bed and breakfast consists of a Swiss-style farmhouse and cottages surrounded by three acres of century-old trees. The property overlooks a two-hundred-acre farm and coop of chickens, ducks, and turkeys. The atmosphere is completely rural, yet Sonoma's town square is less than a mile away.

The farmhouse and cottages are colorfully decorated with hand-painted murals and vintage fabrics, along with California pottery from the forties. Laura's Cottage is particularly delightful, set beneath the huge eucalyptus and pepper trees. But the Honeymoon Cottage is also popular, with its wood stove, loft, and clawfoot tub. All in all, the Sonoma Chalet is a refreshing departure from the plethora of sterile, yuppified bed and breakfasts found throughout the wine country. It's not a luxurious place, but it's Sonoma as it really was.

SONOMA CHALET

Telephone:	**(707) 938-3129**
Address:	**18935 Fifth Street West, Sonoma 95476**
Rates:	**$75 to $135, including breakfast**
Directions:	**From Sonoma's town square, head west on West Napa Street; turn right on Fifth Street West and follow it to the end.**

Sonoma Mission Inn & Spa

In addition to the usual spa pamperings and pummelings offered at the Sonoma Mission Inn, you can also have a personal tarot card reading, guided meditation, or energy balancing treatment here. Since its opening as a bathhouse in 1895 (it burned down twice and was rebuilt in 1927 as a replica of a California mission), this luxury resort has been attracting wealthy weekenders and button-downers from San Francisco. It has never been a hard-core fitness spa, but more of a pampering, mellow-out kind of place. Their natural hot artesian water—said to contain more than twenty-five minerals—is pumped into the pools and whirlpools from a source directly beneath the inn. It claims to be the only four-star luxury resort in the West where you can "take the waters."

SONOMA MISSION INN & SPA

Telephone:	**(800) 862-4945; (707) 938-9000**
Address:	**P.O. Box 1447, Sonoma 95476**
Rates:	**$140 to $625**
Directions:	**in Boyes Hot Springs on SR-12, two miles north of Sonoma.**

YOUNTVILLE

Napa Valley Railway Inn

Railroad buffs will enjoy the Napa Valley Railway Inn, a connected line of nine turn-of-the-century railway cars converted into suites. Guests can choose from among three small cabooses and six more spacious rail cars, each with skylights over the beds. While clean, the interior decor is somewhat uninspiring. But the inn has a great location in picturesque Yountville amid the surrounding vineyards. Vintage 1870, a brick-built maze of quaint shops and cafes, is right next door.

NAPA VALLEY RAILWAY INN

Telephone: **(707) 944-2000**
Address: **6503 Washington Street, Yountville 94599**
Rates: **$65 to $115**
Directions: **From SR-29, take the Yountville exit; turn right on California Drive, then left on Washington Street.**

MENDOCINO AND LAKE COUNTIES

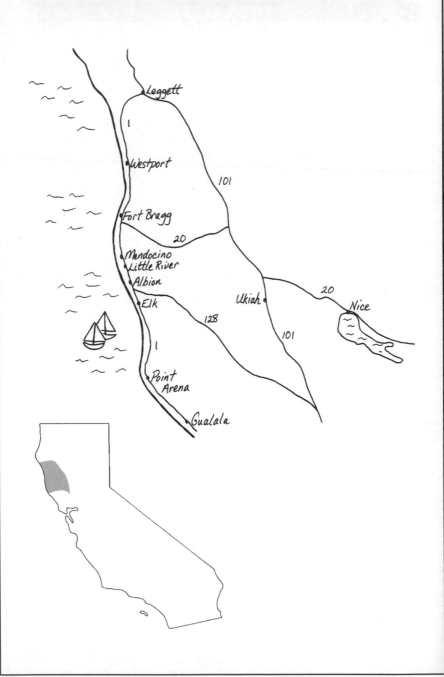

8 MENDOCINO AND LAKE COUNTIES

ALBION

Fensalden Inn

Situated on twenty green acres in the Mendocino coastal foothills, the Fensalden Inn was once a stagecoach way station. In addition to the main house, you can stay in the redwood water tower, which dates back to the 1860s. The most popular of the two water tower units is the Captain's Walk Suite, with striking, timbered cathedral ceilings. It has a wood-burning fireplace in the downstairs sitting room. Also included is a kitchen and upstairs bedroom loft. The water tower's setting, under the shade of a towering Monterey cypress tree, is quite pastoral.

FENSALDEN INN

Telephone: **(707) 937-4042**
Address: **P.O. Box 99, Albion 95410**
Rates: **$95 to $130 (Captain's Walk Suite), including full breakfast and afternoon wine and hors d'oeuvres**
Directions: **seven miles south of Mendocino; from Highway 1, head east on Navarro Ridge Road.**

Albion River Inn

The whole Mendocino coast is one spectacular vista after another, and the Albion River Inn makes sure that no one loses out on the view. Every cottage is lined up along the cliff's edge, affording an unobstructed view of Albion Cove. These are no slouch cottages, either. Decorated in a crisp, upscale country style, they're all clean as a whistle. And, in the spirit of true democracy, everyone gets a fireplace, too.

No matter where I've stayed around here, there are two restaurants that local innkeepers almost always recommend for dinner—Cafe Beaujolais and the Albion River Inn. I have yet to try the latter but can attest that its cliffside location beats any dining room in the area for the view.

ALBION RIVER INN

Telephone:	**(800) 479-7944; (707) 937-1919**
Address:	**P.O. Box 100, Albion 95410**
Rates:	**$160 to $250, including full breakfast**
Directions:	**on Highway 1 in Albion, on the north side of the bridge.**

ELK

Greenwood Pier Inn

A beguiling hostelry, Greenwood Pier Inn makes the most of its stunning location atop an ocean bluff. The myriad rock formations rising out of the sea are a magnificent sight. While the whole coastline of Mendocino is spectacular, this particular view still haunts me.

The inn is comprised of a handful of quirky houses and cottages nestled among flowery gardens. In addition to the main Victorian house and several guest cottages, there's also a country store and garden shop, plus an indoor-outdoor cafe that features herbs and vegetables from the garden.

Each structure has an intriguing design. Owners Kendrick and Isabel Petty, both artists, have added fanciful touches to every nook and cranny. My favorite is Cliffhouse, a redwood cottage hugging the edge of the cliff. It features a private deck, fireplace, and very special Jacuzzi tub. The tub, atop a spiral staircase, has big picture windows that look directly out to sea, with romantic candles ready to light. Sea Castle, which has two units, is also a cliffhanger, with fireplaces and upper-level ocean-view tubs. The other rooms are set back somewhat from the cliff, but they almost all have knockout views.

The sea's rock formations offer a stunning view at Greenwood Pier Inn.

GREENWOOD PIER INN

Telephone: **(707) 877-9997; fax (707) 877-3439**
Address: **5928 South Highway 1, Box 336, Elk 95432**
Rates: **$100 to $225, including continental breakfast**
Directions: **on Highway 1 in Elk.**

FORT BRAGG

LITTLE NOVELTY: Remember our old friend Magic Fingers? **The Surf Motel** in Fort Bragg is one of California's few remaining motels with coin-operated vibrating beds. As for the rest—let's say it's exactly as motels were in the sixties, and leave it at that. For more information, call the Surf Motel, (707) 964- 5361.

St. Orres

Everything about St. Orres is imaginative, from its Russian-inspired copper domes to the playfully presented dinners. Set across from an arresting stretch of coastline just north of Gualala (pronounced "Wah-LAH-lah"), the main lodge resembles a dacha, or country house, with its weathered wood, profusion of stained glass, and rustic filigree. It's a fanciful reminder of former Russian inhabitants who settled in this area to establish their fur trade during the 1800s. This dacha, however, was built in the late seventies by a group of back-to-landers from the Bay Area. They hand-crafted the fantastic structure out of century-old redwood and mostly recycled materials. Gradually, an eclectic collection of eleven cottages—some with their own miniature domes—were built or moved to the wooded slope behind the main lodge.

The rustic, stained-glass, and weathered-wood look of St. Orres offers a reminder of its former Russian occupants.

The lodge guest rooms are up a wooden spiral staircase to the second floor. They all share "his," "hers," and "ours" (with a double-headed shower) baths. Although nicely paneled in wood, most of the lodge rooms are small and poorly ventilated. As for the cottages, they all have their own personalities—from the Pine Haven (with its octagonal bathroom of eight skylights) to the cozy Tree House to Sequoia with its ocean view. Seven of the cottages have exclusive use of a spa facility with a hot tub, sauna, and sun deck.

After two decades, the original owners are still very much here. There's Eric Black, the designer and builder; Ted Black, the manager and "wizard-of-all-works"; and Rosemary Campiformio, their award-winning chef.

Rosemary is the creative hand behind the inn's restaurant, known throughout California for its north-coast cuisine. Her emphasis is on wild things, including boar, Sonoma County quail, pheasant, venison, wild mushrooms, teas (Have you ever had pine needle, wild fennel, or nettle tea?), and fresh local produce. "Everything on the menu can be found here in the area," she says. I had a most memorable dinner in their domed dining room, with its dizzying three stories of leaded glass—an awesome room even without the food. The meal began with a just-out-of-the-oven loaf of rosemary bread and cold cucumber-raisin-walnut soup. The mixed greens were decorated with an apricot vinaigrette and jicama stars. And my seafood surprise—baby steelhead salmon with Dungeness crab, spinach, and wild mushrooms—was wrapped in parchment paper and colorful ribbons, like a birthday present. I didn't have room for dessert, but reliable sources report the *tulipe de praline* is outrageous. Breakfast, delivered to the cottages, is equally rich. To fight off that I-ate-too-much feeling, I took a walk around the grounds, humming "St. Orres in Wah-lah-lah" like a mantra under my breath. Try it—it rolls so exotically off the tongue. Midway through my stroll, a family of deer padded nonchalantly across my path.

ST. ORRES

Telephone: **(707) 884-3303; fax (707) 884-1543**
Address: **36601 Highway 1, P.O. Box 523, Gualala 95445**
Rates: **$60 to $180, including full breakfast**
Directions: **two miles north of Gualala, on Highway 1.**

The Old Milano Hotel

Nestled in a fern-filled meadow next to the Old Milano Hotel is an adorable turn-of-the-century red caboose from the North Pacific Coast Railroad. Inside, all vintage fixtures remain intact. A short ladder leads up to two brakemans' seats with windows looking on to the greenery. In the bedroom there's a pot-belly stove and little deck.

The Victorian-style hotel is almost as romantic, with its stunning location on the cliffs of the southern Mendocino coast. Room Four has the best view in the main house, its picture window overlooking craggy Castle Rock, rising dramatically out of the sea.

If you really want to take advantage of the view, book some private time in the cliff-side hot tub. It's screened off from the hotel, yet open to the sea, so you have complete privacy for au naturel bathing. Bring a bottle of champagne.

All aboard for the Old Milano Hotel, where vintage fixtures remain intact.

THE OLD MILANO HOTEL

Telephone: **(707) 884-3256**
  Address: **38300 Highway 1, Gualala 95445**
    Rates: **$80 to $165, including full breakfast**
Directions: **on Highway 1, one mile north of Gualala.**

LITTLE RIVER

Stevenswood Lodge

Although Stevenswood Lodge has a splendid wooded setting, it is most notable for its sculpture garden and original artwork. The airy interior of white walls and polished wood floors makes an ideal backdrop for the paintings. Indeed, there's even a little art gallery near the entry. Outside, amid the chatter of blue jays and chipmunks, you can wander the grounds and contemplate the sculptural pieces that punctuate the evergreens.

All rooms are suites with fireplaces, cathedral ceilings, and big picture windows facing the forest. It's one of the few totally contemporary lodgings in the Mendocino area.

STEVENSWOOD LODGE

Telephone: **(800) 421-2810; (707) 937-2810**
  Address: **8211 North Highway 1, Little River 95460**
    Rates: **$95 to $195**
Directions: **on Highway 1, a quarter-mile north of Van Damme State Park.**

Heritage House

Heritage House is spread over thirty-seven acres of rugged ocean bluffs and rolling green lawns. There is a boggling array of cottages, with no two alike. Among them, with prime views near the cliff, are "Same Time" and "Next Year"—one cottage divided into two units. None of the cottages actually hang over the cliff—on the contrary, they're all set safely back from the edge. But the Same Time, Next Year, Meadow, and Seacliff cottages come pretty darned close, and they have the best views. Of the many other guest units, there's also a water tower—an omnipresent sight in Mendocino—converted into a suite.

The main house, which dates back to 1877, is built in the New England style so pervasive in this area. (Interesting to note that the descendants of the original owners, the Dennens, still own the inn today.) The guests are largely on the conservative side, and jackets are requested in their somewhat dated dining room. The whole inn has a restrained, East Coast air. You won't see anyone gamboling about with unchecked abandon on the grounds. A slow, dignified stroll is the general pace here.

HERITAGE HOUSE

Telephone: **(800) 235-5885; (707) 937-5885**
Address: **5200 North Highway 1, Little River 95456**
Rates: **$180 to $350, including dinner and breakfast for two**
Directions: **on Highway 1, at the south end of Little River.**

Glendeven Inn

A long-established inn next to Van Damme State Park, Glendeven Inn has it own art gallery. Built into the bottom level of a former hayloft (the entire second floor is a guest suite), the gallery sits opposite the farmhouse-style inn. The artwork, most of which is the work of Northwest artists, includes a beautiful collection of contemporary paintings, ceramics, and jewelry. Also on display are handcrafted furnishings designed and built by the inn's Dutch-born owner, Jan de Vries.

The guest rooms are airy, tasteful, and unfussy. But the gallery is worth seeing whether or not you stay here.

GLENDEVEN INN

Telephone: **(707) 937-0083; fax (707) 937-6108**
Address: **8221 North Highway 1, Little River 95456**
Rates: **$70 to $275, including full breakfast and afternoon wine**
Directions: **on Highway 1, a quarter-mile north of Van Damme State Park.**

See the "Chicken Hilton," the fanciest chicken coop in the West, at Brewery Gulch Inn.

MENDOCINO

Brewery Gulch Inn

At the Brewery Gulch Inn, instead of the usual mint by your bed, you get a little bag of chicken seed accompanied by a sign: "For your chicken-feeding pleasure."

Wander out back and sure enough, there's the chicken coop. But it's not just any chicken coop—it's a veritable Chicken Hilton. It was years ago that owner Arky Ciancutti told me the story behind this coop, so the details are a bit fuzzy. But I believe it stems back to one moonlit night when Arky's friends dared him to build the fanciest chicken coop in the West. I think a bottle of tequila was somewhere in the story, too. But Arky never does anything half-way. He built the darned thing, complete with undulating roof and mullioned windows. When my mother saw a photo of the coop, she assumed it was a guest cottage.

Arky, a former physician, has also gone full tilt with his garden at Brewery Gulch, which was featured in *Home Garden*. He spends more than forty hours a week on his twelve acres, caring for six hundred rhododendrons, one thousand ferns, and his award-winning varieties of rose bushes. Every year he plants more than three thousand bulbs. It's not a symmetrical, orderly kind of garden. The pathway to the house, for instance, leads across a soft green lawn covered with pines and creeping passion flowers. Bird houses dangle from the tree branches, while hummingbirds hover over the fuschias. It's an enchanting, magical space.

Built in 1854, Brewery Gulch qualifies as the oldest ranch in Mendocino County. The farmhouse has five guest rooms which the brochure describes as "down-home and unpretentious." They're not kidding—after the lush display outside, the bedrooms seem quite modest.

BREWERY GULCH INN

Telephone:	**(707) 937-4752**
Address:	**9350 Coast Highway 1, Mendocino 95460**
Rates:	**$85 to $130, including full breakfast (with eggs from the resident chickens)**
Directions:	**on Highway 1, just south of Mendocino.**

The Stanford Inn by the Sea

Jeff Stanford describes his place as "more of a garden with an inn than an inn with a garden." He's right. The Stanford Inn by the Sea is not just an inn—it's an entire eco-compound. Spread over ten acres of land directly across the river from Mendocino, the property contains three different Stanford family businesses: a certified organic nursery, a canoe and mountain-bike shop, and the inn. Oh, and eight resident llamas, fourteen cats, numerous horses, dogs, and black swans. Everything coexists peacefully.

In fact, this is one of the most environmentally sensitive lodgings I have ever encountered. Fresh produce from the garden is used for breakfast; any leftovers go into a compost pile. Guests can take complimentary classes on organic gardening and medicinal herbs. The dried flowers from the nursery are made into wreaths for the guest rooms (which also contain live plants and flowers). Even the llama dung goes into a compost pile. (As you can imagine, these compost piles are no small heaps.) As Jeff showed me around the grounds, he pointed out the spots he and his wife Joan had intentionally left natural, allowing the weeds to grow for the frogs and wild creatures. (The property has become a haven for animals—even gophers are allowed to stay.) A circular "Eye of Horus" herb garden near the entry is in the works.

With its rural setting and New Age flavor, one would assume that the rooms might be kind of rustic, but they're not. Housed in a long lodge built of dark wood, they're all luxuriously romantic, with four-poster or sleigh beds, inviting burgundy velvet love seats, cozy wood paneling, fireplaces, and ocean-view balconies. Each room is a bit different, but they all come equipped with telephones, televisions, VCRs, robes, and a welcome split of wine. Melt-in-your-mouth cake is served in the lobby every afternoon, followed by wine and hors d'oeuvres, and then a hearty breakfast (with organic coffee) in the morning. A lap pool, sauna, and hot tub are enclosed by a huge greenhouse-like structure. Every Wednesday, yoga classes are held by the pool.

Two of the eight resident llamas at Stanford Inn by the Sea are at home on ten acres.

Those who need still more to do can take a canoe or kayak up the river. Their Catch a Canoe and Bicycles, Too! shop has some special redwood canoes unlike any others. They also rent out mountain bikes and in-line skates for short jaunts into Mendocino.

THE STANFORD INN BY THE SEA

Telephone: **(800) 331-8884; (707) 937-5615; fax (707) 937-0305**
Address: **Highway 1 and Comptche-Ukiah Road, P.O. Box 487, Mendocino 95460**
Rates: **$175 to $275, including full breakfast, afternoon wine, and hors d'oeuvres; pets welcome**
Directions: **just south of downtown Mendocino, at Highway 1 and Comptche-Ukiah Road.**

Captain's Cove Inn

Formerly known as 1021 Main Street, Captain's Cove Inn is in downtown Mendocino, right on the bluffs, with a path leading directly down to a sandy beach. The 1861 home also has several eclectic guest buildings. Next door is Driftwood, a tin-roofed A-frame that was formerly an artist's foundry. Its sleeping loft offers an ocean view. Cove Cottage, closest to the ocean, has a private deck, wood-burning stove, and Oriental touches throughout. And Crow's Nest, built over an 1851 barn, also looks intriguing.

Before new owners Bob and Linda Blum took it over, this inn had a reputation for eccentricity. Fans of the former inn should be forewarned that the decor has since been toned down and mainstreamed a bit.

CAPTAIN'S COVE INN

Telephone: **(800) 780-7905**
Address: **44781 Main Street, P.O. Box 803, Mendocino 95460**
Rates: **$125 to $185, including full breakfast**
Directions: **From Highway 1, exit at Main Street and head west for one block.**

John Dougherty House

Mendocino is brimming with historic water towers, many converted into guest accommodations. Of all the water tower lodgings I saw, the most impressive is part of the John Dougherty House. Connected to the main house, it's a two-story tower with artistic touches on the exterior. Inside, the eighteen-foot beamed ceiling hovers above a four-poster bed and hand-stenciled walls. The sitting area has a wood-burning stove. A full breakfast is served in the main house. Built in 1867, the house is among the oldest in Mendocino.

JOHN DOUGHERTY HOUSE

Telephone:	(707) 937-5266
Address:	571 Ukiah Street, P.O. Box 017, Mendocino 95460
Rates:	$95 to $115 for the Water Tower, including full breakfast
Directions:	From Highway 1, exit at Main Street and head west; turn right on Kasten and left on Ukiah.

Joshua Grindle Inn

Joshua Grindle Inn, long considered one of the most reliably good bed and breakfasts in Mendocino, has a redwood water tower with three guest rooms. It stands thirty feet tall behind the inn amid century-old cypress trees. Of the three bedrooms, Water-tower II is especially popular. (Note the absence of art on the walls—pictures don't hang well on a wall that slants inward.) Like Watertower I on the first level, this room features pine furnishings and an old-fashioned wood-burning fireplace.

JOSHUA GRINDLE INN

Telephone:	(800) GRINDLE; (707) 937-4143
Address:	44800 Little Lake Road, P.O. Box 647, Mendocino 95460
Rates:	$95 to $155, including full breakfast
Directions:	From Highway 1, exit at Little Lake Road and head west.

Sweetwater Gardens

The 1872 water tower at Sweetwater Gardens is unique because it has an eight-foot hot tub and sauna at its base. There's only one catch: Because Sweetwater Gardens is also a small spa, day visitors

Go back in time to the western frontier at Blackberry Inn.

share the water tower's sauna, hot tub, and bathroom from early afternoon to late evening. After hours, guests have these facilities to themselves. Even if you don't stay here, this is an atmospheric place for a massage and hot tub. (Ask about their "Rub-a-Dub" specials.) It's right in town, next to Cafe Beaujolais.

SWEETWATER GARDENS

Telephone: **(800) 300-4140; (707) 937-4140**
Address: **955 Ukiah Street, P.O. Box 337, Mendocino 95460**
Rates: **$84 to $94**
Directions: **From Highway 1, exit at Main Street and head west; turn right on Evergreen, then left on Ukiah.**

Blackberry Inn

Blackberry Inn is a little motel that's built like a western frontier town on the outside, with each connecting guest cottage representing a different, turn-of-the-century shop. Among the various rooms are the Bank, Millinery (complete with hats in the window), Sheriff, Barber Shop, Saloon, and Gazette. Inside, the rooms are conventionally decorated with safe, neutral-colored furnishings. They're not, however, without their luxuries—wood-burning fireplaces or stoves, ocean views (across Highway One), and some Roman tubs, to name a few. Belle's Place is the most romantic choice.

BLACKBERRY INN

Telephone:	**(707) 937-5281**
Address:	**44051 Larkin Road, Mendocino 95460**
Rates:	**$85 to $135**
Directions:	**From Highway 1, on the north side of Mendocino, head east on Larkin Road.**

NICE

Featherbed Railroad Company

Of several railroad lodgings in California, the Featherbed Railroad Company is the most romantic. These cabooses are charmingly restored, and the interiors are equally inviting.

The railroad cars, from the Southern Pacific and Santa Fe Railroads, stand on individual segments of track in a zigzag pattern amid a cool, tree-shaded lawn. Directly across the road is lovely Clear Lake. A tree swing, hammock, red British phone booth, and old-fashioned lampposts hung with flower pots add to the sentimental setting. In the back of the five-acre property is a swimming pool and century-old ranch house which serves as the innkeeper's living quarters. After breakfast on the verandah, guests can go for a spin on the inn's bicycle built for two.

The nine railroad cars are decorated in different, sometimes seductive themes. Casablanca (which comes with a little piano), Orient Express, and La Loose Caboose are the most requested and exotic cars. All three feature large, mirrored Jacuzzi tubs with fragrant soaps and rubber duckies. Wild Wild West is full of western memorabilia. Its bar even has a brass footrail and poker game at the ready. Other cars such as Rosebud and Mint Julep are done in frilly bed and breakfast decor. The only car dedicated strictly to railroading is Casey Jones, less romantic than the others. Painted red, white, and blue, Casey Jones is equipped with a cupola and train gear, including an engineer's cap and coveralls.

The bay window alcoves of some cabooses have been turned into dining areas, with coffeemakers, chocolates, and mugs set at the table. The antiques, wall coverings, morning paper at your door—they're among the many touches that set Featherbed above the other railroad lodgings.

FEATHERBED RAILROAD COMPANY

Telephone: **(800) 966-6322; (707) BR GUEST**
  Address: **2870 Lakeshore Boulevard, P.O. Box 4016, Nice 95464**
    Rates: **$90 to $140, including continental breakfast**
Directions: **off SR-20, in the southwest side of Nice, on Clear Lake.**

POINT ARENA

Point Arena Lighthouse

Although the original structure was destroyed in the San Francisco earthquake of 1906, Point Arena Lighthouse has been guiding boats with its beacon since 1870. Rebuilt in 1908, the 115-foot concrete tower stands out along this narrow, desolate promontory of the south Mendocino coast. For a small fee, day visitors can tour the museum and climb to the lighthouse. But you can also spend a couple of nights in one of several nearby vacation homes. The rentals provide income for site maintenance, as no government funding is extended. Each house (more than a tad boring) has three bedrooms, two baths, a fully stocked kitchen, and a living room with wood stove. Guests bring their own sheets and towels. Because one house accommodates as many as six people, the $120 group rate is a good deal for families. But for just two people . . . you'd have to be a lighthouse buff.

POINT ARENA LIGHTHOUSE

Telephone: **(707) 882-2777**
Address: **P.O. Box 11, Point Arena 95468**
Rate: **$90 for one or two people; $120 for three to six; two-night minimum required**
Directions: **Just north of Point Arena on Highway 1, look for Lighthouse Road on the left.**

UKIAH

Vichy Hot Springs Resort

Here's a locale that offers the only naturally carbonated warm mineral springs in North America. People have been drawn to these healing, effervescent waters since the time of the ancient Pomo Indians. Some old locals around Vichy still attribute their longevity to this fizzy water. The "champagne baths" were a favorite retreat of Mark Twain, Jack London, Ulysses S. Grant, and Teddy Roosevelt. Back in the hot Victorian summers, they rode the train up to Ukiah and then hopped a horse-drawn carriage to Vichy. The original 1860 concrete tubs are still used, although today's guests more often are movie executives or rock musicians.

Marjorie and Gilbert Ashoff, who spent years restoring the spa from utter disrepair (which included removing twenty-five tons of scrap metal), have since transformed Vichy into a delightful bed and breakfast resort. Their reception building and guest quarters, which consist of a long, nineteenth-century building and two 1854 cottages, are set around a broad, tree-shaded lawn. The cottages—Mendocino County's oldest standing structures—are always in demand, but the other bedrooms have a fresh, endearing simplicity. The wood floors, tubs, and concrete showers are all original.

Across the lawn is an Olympic-sized swimming pool. There's a nice play area with a fort, soccer field, and tetherball available to children of the guests. The Ashoffs welcome families here. Their daughter, Annelies, grew up at Vichy Springs and works at the resort when she's home from college.

The massage building, hot tub, and mineral baths are down a gravel pathway and over an arched, Giverny-like bridge. (Indeed, it is a duplicate of Monet's bridge.) The masseuses are excellent ("As part of their interview, they have to give both of us a massage," Marjorie says with a smile), and the tubs are blissful. Each tub—some are enclosed for privacy—is long enough to hold one floating individual. They're ingeniously designed—you just pull out the metal stopper and let the fresh spring water rush in.

The resort is surrounded by seven hundred acres of natural terrain—a haven for hikers and experienced mountain bikers. Unfortunately, it's also a haven for poison oak. But no need to worry—the mineral springs can reportedly cure that, too.

Vichy Springs is open to day visitors.

VICHY HOT SPRINGS RESORT

Telephone: **(707) 462-9515; fax (707) 462-9516**
Address: **2605 Vichy Springs Road, Ukiah 95482**
Rates: **$89 to $165, including full breakfast**
Directions: **From US-101, exit at Vichy Springs Road, and follow historic landmark signs three miles east to resort.**

Vichy Hot Springs Resort offers North America's only naturally carbonated warm mineral springs.

Orr Hot Springs

This natural mineral springs retreat is fourteen winding miles west of Highway 101 in the rolling foothills of Mendocino County.

After crossing a footbridge over the creek, a tall log gate conceals rustic forties redwood cabins and campsites in the natural ravine. A nice woman with shaved head and pierced nose might guide you through flowery pathways to the bathhouses. The silky mineral springs flow into individual porcelain bathtubs and a wonderful swimming pool built directly into the rock. You bring your own food and cook in a communal kitchen.

Orr Hot Springs is much like Stewart Mineral Springs in its general layout, but the overtones here are even earthier. Guests are allowed to bathe au naturel. Some wear red "silence beads" if they don't want anyone talking to them. The pool is inviting, but the tubs, around since 1863, have seen better days. Orr Hot Springs is for those adventurous souls who really want to get in touch with nature in every way.

ORR HOT SPRINGS

Telephone:	**(707) 462-6277**
Address:	**13201 Orr Springs Road, Ukiah 95482**
Rates:	**$25 to $122**
Directions:	**From US-101 at Ukiah, exit at North State Street and head north; turn left on Orr Springs Road and continue for thirteen and one-half miles.**

WESTPORT

Howard Creek Ranch

A former sheep and cattle ranch from the 1800s, Howard Creek Ranch encompasses forty rural acres that sweep from the hillside beneath the Highway 1 bridge to a sandy beach. The New England-style farmhouse is traditional enough, with country antiques and handmade quilts in the bedrooms. Things get more interesting once you cross the seventy-five-foot swinging bridge spanning Howard Creek. On this side of the bridge are a quirky collection of barns and cabins, most of which have a rustic kind of charm. Meadow Cabin, for instance, has its own outhouse. And the Boat—well, you have to see it to believe it. Tucked among the trees next to the creek, it's a redwood cabin built around the hull of a boat. The cabin and boat blend together so well it's hard to tell where one begins and the other ends. But inside you can clearly see the outline of the former galley where the present kitchen exists. A personal favorite is the Beach House, a redwood cabin with a private deck, skylights, and homey, handcrafted interior. It's set back about two hundred yards from the beach, but you can still spot a bit of the ocean.

A massage cabin with hot tub, sauna, and a German masseuse is on top of the mountain overlooking the whole spread. Innkeepers Charles and Sally Grigg also offer horse-drawn wagon rides at the ranch.

HOWARD CREEK RANCH

Telephone:	**(707) 964-6725**
Address:	**40501 North Highway 1, P.O. Box 121, Westport 95488**
Rates:	**$80 to $145, including full breakfast; pets are welcome**
Directions:	**on Highway 1, three miles north of Westport.**

Howard Creek Ranch was a sheep and cattle ranch in the 1800s.

9 THE FAR NORTH

Clearwater House

If you've read and watched *A River Runs Through It* too often, then it's time for a visit to Clearwater House, a northeastern California inn catering exclusively to fly fishermen. They offer two-to five-day schools for all skill levels of angling, from beginner to advanced. It's the only lodging in California officially endorsed by Orvis, the purveyors of gentlemanly fishing.

The pristine white stucco farmhouse, built at the turn of the century, has an anteroom for removing your waders. The back lawn is used for casting practice. Scattered throughout the somewhat spartan but comfortable living room and library are books on, what else, fly-fishing. When I visited the inn during the day, no guests were around—they were off on fishing excursions or practicing their angling on Hat Creek bordering the farmhouse. Everyone talks trout during the family-style meals.

Clearwater House welcomes nonfishermen as well—spouses who come just to relax, for instance. But there's not a whole lot else to do in this remote corner of the state. During the trout season, from late April to mid-November, the focus is solely on fishing.

CLEARWATER HOUSE

Telephone: **from November through April (off season): (415) 381-1173; fax (415) 383-9136**
Telephone: **from May to October (in season): (916) 335-5500**
Reservations: **274 Star Route, Muir Beach 94965**
Rates: **$110 per person, including breakfast; $140 per person, including three meals; ask about their angling packages**
Directions: **in Cassel, four miles south of SR-299.**

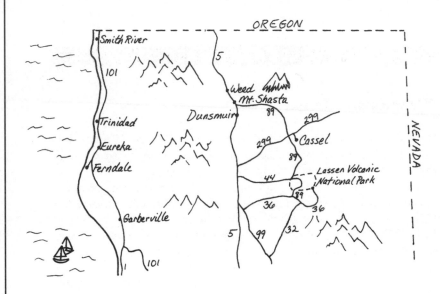

Caboose Motel/Railroad Park Resort

Railroad Park Resort is a whole resort complex based at the foot
of scenic Castle Crags near Mt. Shasta. On the grounds are antique
dining cars, cabins, a campground, RV park, and the Caboose
Motel—a collection of cabooses from the old Southern Pacific,
Santa Fe, and Great Northern lines. Their interiors have been converted into motel rooms, with painted or knotty cedar paneling,
miniblinds, and brass beds. Gathered in a loose circle around the
swimming pool, they make a colorful display against the striking
mountain backdrop. When making reservations, ask for a caboose
on the inside perimeter. Those on the outside are plunked down
on the parking lot asphalt like RVs, with no landscaping.

CABOOSE MOTEL/RAILROAD PARK RESORT

Telephone:	**(800) 974-RAIL (in CA); (916) 235-4440; fax (916) 235-4470**
Address:	**100 Railroad Park Road, Dunsmuir 96025**
Rates:	**$70 to $85**
Directions:	**From I-5, exit at Railroad Park.**

The Caboose Motel's railroad cars are gathered in a loose circle around a swimming pool.

An Elegant Victorian Mansion

This is not just a bed and breakfast: An Elegant Victorian Mansion is an immersion into living history. From the moment innkeeper Doug Vieyra greets you at the door in his butler costume ("I'm Jeeves, your impeccable butler!" he says), you leave the twentieth century behind.

When I first toured this inn, it had not yet opened and was bereft of any furnishings. Doug and his wife, Lily, led me from room to room, animatedly describing every detail, what would go here and there. Their enthusiasm was infectious, and I was eager to see what the finished mansion would look like. Upon my return five years later, I was astonished by the transformation. Their three parlors and library are exquisitely detailed with hand-painted moldings, intricately pieced Bradbury and Bradbury wall-paper (nearly three hundred pieces per room), rich draperies with century-old trim, Oriental rugs—all alive with texture. And despite the fact that Doug and Lily have run the entire inn by themselves all these years, their enthusiasm hasn't waned one bit.

They love dressing in turn-of-the-century costumes and cranking up the gramophone with popular tunes of the era. All two hundred of their cassettes play old-fashioned music. The five hundred videos, some of which are silent films, have vintage themes. Their books deal with Victorian housekeeping and archi-tecture. Pick up a magazine or newspaper from the table and its dateline might be 1905. They even use twenty-five-watt bulbs in the lamps to simulate gaslight.

Outside, the garden is filled with flowers commonly grown in Victorian times. You can play croquet, ride around historic Eureka on complimentary bicycles, or go for a spin in Doug's Model A Ford. In the morning, the dining room table is set for-mally, as a Victorian table would be, with place cards for each guest.

The upstairs guest rooms are named after nineteenth-century notables, including two—Lillie Langtry and Leland Stan-ford, Jr.—who stayed in these very rooms. In the shared bathroom is an authentic pull-chain toilet. Downstairs, there are two more bathrooms, with a Finnish sauna and double-head shower.

An Elegant Victorian Mansion innkeepers Doug and Lily Vieyra pull out all the stops in making you feel at home.

My teenaged niece, who stayed here with me, loves this inn more than any lodging on the California coast. She put on her shawl and derby hat and really got into it, much to the delight of Doug and Lily. In the evening, we played a rousing game of vintage scrabble in the library and, after finishing deadlocked, we replaced the tiles the way they had first read:

```
      G
      R   T
    WELCOME
      E       L
      T       E
      I       G
      N       A   M
      G       N   A
      S   VICTORIAN
                  S
                  I
                  O
                  N
```

AN ELEGANT VICTORIAN MANSION

Telephone: **(707) 444-3144; (707) 442-5594**
Address: **Fourteenth and C Streets, Eureka 95501**
Rates: **$115 to $145, including full breakfast**
Directions: **From US-101, head south on C Street to Fourteenth Street.**

Carter House

Carter House has come a long way from its days as a three-room bed and breakfast in Eureka. It's now one of the most upscale inns along the northern coast, with more than thirty rooms in three different Victorian buildings. There's also a fine, full-service restaurant, elaborate organic garden, and extensive wine cellar.

The restaurant's twenty-five-page wine list will give you a good idea of what the Carter House is all about. If that doesn't grab you, visit the wine shop, where you will find a selection of ten thousand bottles representing eight hundred different wines. During the cocktail hour, guests can sample some of these wines with hors d'oeuvres in the light, airy lounge of the main hotel.

The inn consists of three Victorian-style buildings—the original Carter House, the Bell Cottage, and the Hotel Carter—right across the street from each other. The original Carter House is a three-story, dark redwood structure that looks old but was actually built from the ground up by innkeepers Mark and Christi Carter. Some rooms feature fireplaces and huge whirlpool tubs for two.

As nice as they are, however, the Carter House rooms seem almost secondary to the focus on food and wine. The restaurant emphasizes local seafood and has been praised by all the major food critics. The complimentary breakfasts have been rated by *California* magazine as the best in California. Among their specialties: eggs benedict with Black Forest ham, apple-almond phyllo tarts, warm fruit muffins, and poached pears in wine sauce.

All of the produce is culled from the inn's organic garden, which grows more than three hundred varieties of herbs, greens, vegetables, and edible flowers. Every afternoon, guests are invited out to the garden to help the chefs collect produce for the evening meal. The Carter House also hosts organic gardening seminars and tours by the master gardener.

CARTER HOUSE

Telephone: **(800) 404-1390; (707) 445-1390; fax (707) 444-8062**
Address: **301 L Street, Eureka 95501**
Rates: **$125 to $275, including breakfast and afternoon wine and hors d'oeuvres**
Directions: **From US-101 in downtown Eureka, head north on L Street.**

FERNDALE

Gingerbread Mansion Inn

Ferndale is a showcase of colorful, well-preserved Victorian homes, and the Gingerbread Mansion Inn is one of its most photographed. Painted yellow and orange with turrets, balconies, and ornate gingerbread trim, it's an architectural gem.

The bathrooms are particularly memorable. The bathroom in the Rose Suite, for instance, has a corner fireplace, large claw-foot tub, and mirrored walls and ceilings. In the Gingerbread Suites, "his" and "hers" tubs are positioned toe-to-toe in the bed-room. The Fountain Suite has a truly deluxe bathroom with a fainting couch and twin, side-by-side clawfoot tubs on a raised platform before the tiled fireplace. The pièce de résistance is the newly built Empire Suite—a stunning room with dramatically pitched ceilings and Roman columns. Off to one side is a fire-place with full living and dining area. On the other side is an oversized porcelain tub in front of a second fireplace. The shower is spectacular—all marble, with three shower heads and five sepa-rate massage sprays coming at you from all directions.

GINGERBREAD MANSION INN

Telephone: **(800) 952-4136; (707) 786-4000; fax (707) 786-4381**
Address: **400 Berding Street, P.O. Box 40, Ferndale 95536**
Rates: **$140 to $350, including full breakfast and afternoon tea**
Directions: **From US-101, take the Ferndale exit and follow Main Street into town; turn left at the Bank of America.**

GARBERVILLE

Benbow Inn

The Tudor architecture and bucolic riverside setting of the Benbow Inn serve as a fitting backdrop for fanciful seasonal events. In May, for instance, a Teddy Bear Tea offers everyone a chance to dress up and bring their favorite bears. Every July during the Shakespeare festival at Benbow Lake, the inn hosts "Bad Shakespeare" poetry contests. For Christmas, they go all out with at least four decorated trees in the lobby, live entertainment every night, and a seven-course Christmas Day dinner. Throughout the year are murder-mystery weekends.

The lobby is particularly handsome, with carved wood archways, tapestry furnishings, Oriental carpets over wood floors, and unfinished checkers and jigsaw puzzles set up at little tables. Every afternoon an English tea is served to the guests.

This 1926 inn is near the gateway to the Avenue of the Giants, an enchanted, thirty-mile drive through the redwoods. Not to be missed.

BENBOW INN

Telephone: **(800) 355-3301; (707) 923-2124; fax (707) 923-2897**
Address: **445 Lake Benbow Drive, Garberville 95542**
Rates: **$110 to $200, including afternoon tea and evening hors d'oeuvres**
Directions: **From US-101, exit at Benbow Drive.**

LASSEN NATIONAL PARK

Drakesbad Guest Ranch

Set in a beautiful, high alpine valley in Lassen National Park, Drakesbad Guest Ranch is the ultimate, mountain getaway— unspoiled and timeless. Granted, it's remote: After winding your way over to Lake Almanor, you wind farther into the south side of the park. The last three miles are dirt road. But it's worth every mile.

Bungalows One through Six—the most requested accommodations—are quintessential mountain cabins. Facing a wide meadow and the forested peaks beyond, they're cheerful and light, with log-framed beds and warm wood walls. Old-style metal chairs (the kind my grandma used to have on the porch of her thirties home) sit on the wooden decks.

Open for 110 years, Drakesbad still has no electricity apart from a daytime generator for the kitchen and dining room. When I was there, the rooms and lodge were glowing at night with romantic kerosene lamps. But host Ed Fiebiger told me the fire department would soon require them to find a safer, less attractive means of lighting.

Aside from horseback riding (a basket of carrots is always by the door of the dining hall to feed the horses), fishing, hiking, and the enjoyment of nature, a big highlight at Drakesbad is its hot, spring-fed swimming pool, a short stroll through the meadow. The water temperature is naturally ninety-five to one hundred degrees, and guests are welcome to take a dip any time of the day or night.

There's such a good feeling here, many guests book for the following year before they depart. As a result, 80 percent of their clientele are return guests. The season—from June to October—is short, so be sure to schedule well in advance. Reaching the ranch by phone in season is tricky because Drakesbad can only be accessed by a toll station. Call in the winter, or write.

DRAKESBAD GUEST RANCH

Telephone: **In summer, Drakesbad Toll Station Number 2. (Contact your long distance operator and request to be connected with the Susanville operator in Area Code 916; only this operator can reach the Drakesbad toll stations.) During winter, call (916) 529-1512, or fax (916) 529-4511, or write to 2150 North Main Street, Suite 5, Red Bluff 96080 for reservations; closed October to May**

Rates: **$87.50 to $110 per person, including three meals per day**

Directions: **From Chester, turn north on Feather River Road (at the fire station); the last three miles are gravel. Park entrance fee is $5.**

LEGGETT

Bell Glen Bed & Breakfast and Eel River Redwoods Hostel

Let's start with the Bell Glen Bed & Breakfast, one of the few exceptions to the ugly-cabin syndrome that pervades this state. The cabins here are charming both inside and out. Situated on ten wooded acres next to the Eel River, all six units are romantically decorated with antiques and fresh country accents. Some have Jacuzzi tubs for two (Cabin E has a private outdoor hot tub), four-poster canopy beds, and decks with river views. Each comes with a complimentary bottle of wine, breakfast provisions, and nice touches such as marshmallows and bubble bath. It's obvious hosts Gene and Sandy Barnett have worked hard to create a special experience.

The Barnetts also run the Eel River Redwoods Hostel on the same property. Hostel accommodations range from cabins to shared dorm rooms to a tepee for the overflow. Breakfast is free, and you make it yourself in the communal kitchen. They call it "bunk and breakfast." Pretty ritzy for a hostel.

Up the hillside, in an old building that was once a stage-coach stop, is their rathskeller-style restaurant and pub. The pub is fun, festooned with international flags (and beers) representing all their guests from around the world. On Saturday nights, a "Name That Flag" contest is held.

Bell Glen would make a great base for exploring the sur-rounding redwoods. To that end, Gene has put together a list of self-guided eco-tours.

**BELL GLEN BED & BREAKFAST AND
EEL RIVER REDWOODS HOSTEL**

Telephone: **(707) 925-6425; fax (707) 925-6425**
Address: **70400 Highway 101, Leggett 95585**
Rates: **$95 to $140, including breakfast and wine**
Directions: **on US-101, two miles north of Leggett.**

MOUNT SHASTA

Strawberry Valley Inn

As gorgeous as the scenery is in northeastern California, you won't find a lot of inspired lodgings to match. Strawberry Valley Inn is a charming exception to the run-of-the-mill motels in this region. The delightfully converted motor inn is a flower-filled oasis along Mount Shasta's main drag. An inviting stone reception building snuggles cozily among the tall maple trees and banks of colorful marigolds and petunias. When I arrived here late in the afternoon, guests were enjoying wine out on the patio, with a fantastic view of snow-covered Mount Shasta before them. In the morning, the comforting aroma of baked apples and cinnamon wafted from the breakfast room.

The bedrooms, lined up in the traditional motor inn L-shape, are furnished in rather sterile bed and breakfast decor. It's the exterior of this inn that makes it so unique. With rates starting at fifty dollars, it's a great value.

STRAWBERRY VALLEY INN

Telephone: **(916) 926-2052**
  Address: **1142 South Mount Shasta Boulevard, Mount Shasta 96067**
    Rates: **$49.50 to $68.50, including continental breakfast and afternoon wine**
Directions: **From I-5, take Central Mount Shasta exit (Lake Street) and head east; turn right on Mount Shasta Boulevard and continue south for one-half mile.**

SMITH RIVER

LITTLE NOVELTY: The **Ship Ashore Resort** is a landmark you can't miss on your way through Crescent City—its gift shop is inside a huge, grounded, red, white, and blue yacht. If you're searching for tacky souvenirs to take home with you, look no farther. For more information, call (800) 487-3141 or (707) 487-3141.

TRINIDAD

The Lost Whale Inn

Whenever anyone asks me to name my favorite bed and breakfast in California, the Lost Whale Inn is among the first places that come to mind. If it weren't so inconveniently located way up on the far northern coast, I'd go there at least once a year. I would bring a good book and just sit in an Adirondack chair on the cliff's edge, listening to the crashing waves and sea lions barking on the rocks below. I'd then perhaps descend their 160 steep steps to Abalone Cove, where the rocks have been polished smooth from the incessant pounding of the sea. A sublime dinner at Larrupin Cafe, down the road in Trinidad, would be followed by a late-night hot tub under the stars. Under my cozy quilt, I would drift off to sleep, lulled by the distant sound of the sea lions.

This Cape Cod-style inn was built in 1989 by Susanne Lakin and Lee Miller, two vivacious young artists who fell in love with these four acres of cliff-side, pine-covered land. They designed their inn from scratch, using a house from the back of a

Mozart record jacket for inspiration. It has a fresh, airy feel throughout, with lots of panoramic windows and high, angled ceilings. Downstairs, the Great Room is warmed by amber-colored Douglas fir floors and a wood-burning stove. Upstairs, several of the guest rooms have their own balconies with ethereal views of the ocean through the pine trees. A personal favorite is the Beluga Whale Room on the corner.

Not only is the Lost Whale romantic for couples, it is equally fun for families. I've rarely encountered a bed and breakfast so welcoming to kids. Susanne and Lee, who have two children themselves, designed several bedrooms with extra lofts and sound insulated walls. And if your kids tire of exploring the tidepools or watching the whales and sea lions (Turtle Rock, just below, is one of the largest sea lion rookeries in northern California), they can play on the swing or romp in a custom-built playhouse (complete with loft, heat, and light) out on the sloping lawn. The next cove north is Patrick's Point State Park, known for its veritable treasure chest of polished agates and jade—a rock collector's dream.

Susanne and Lee recently bought a second oceanfront property that will eventually become a guest annex. For now, it houses the dozens of pygmy goats Susanne raises. They also offer weekend seminars on such eclectic topics as screenwriting, rare book collecting, and computer music.

THE LOST WHALE INN

Telephone: **(800) 677-7859; (707) 677-3425; fax (707) 677-0284**
Address: **3452 Patrick's Point Drive, Trinidad 95570**
Rates: **$95 to $140, including afternoon wine and full breakfast**
Directions: **From Highway 1, exit at Patrick's Point Drive and head south one mile.**

WEED

Stewart Mineral Springs

Tucked into a thickly wooded ravine with a creek tumbling through, Stewart Mineral Springs is a clean, New Age retreat with good vibes. The grounds are scattered with guest cabins, motel units, tepees, and lots of open decks and footbridges leading across the creek.

Aside from its tranquil location, most people come here for the natural mineral springs, reputed to have strong healing powers. In a cheery bathhouse are thirteen individual bathing rooms with small, old-fashioned tubs where you can soak in the heated water and relax to healing music. (Alternate the mineral baths with trips to the sauna and dips in the creek.) Massage, polarity therapy, and facials are also offered.

Every Saturday night a Karuk medicine man conducts a Native American purification ceremony in the sweat lodge. Lava rocks, heated for hours, are brought into the lodge amid much fanfare and beating of drums; then water is thrown on them to emit steam. Sometimes the ceremony goes on for hours, or as long as everyone can stand to sweat.

STEWART MINERAL SPRINGS

Telephone:	**(800) 322-9223; (916) 938-2222**
Address:	**4617 Stewart Springs Road, Weed 96094**
Rates:	**$15 to $65; bring your own food**
Directions:	**From I-5, exit at Edgewood (north of Weed) and head east; turn right on Stewart Springs Road and continue for four miles.**

10 NORTHERN SIERRAS

The Coloma Country Inn

Can't decide between ballooning and white-water rafting? How about white-water ballooning? At the Coloma Country Inn, innkeeper Alan Ehrgott will, by prior arrangement, take guests on hot-air balloon rides over the south fork of the American River, skimming the basket right over the rapids. He launches the balloon from behind the farmhouse inn, picturesquely set in the historic gold rush village of Coloma. As the sun rises, you float peacefully over the Sierra foothills, gazing down at the site where gold was first discovered.

That's the other thing that makes this inn unique—it's in the heart of three-hundred-acre Marshall Gold Discovery State Park, preserved much as it was in the 1800s. Horse-drawn carriages clop past the inn, and just a short stroll down the road you can watch demonstrations in the blacksmith and tinsmith shops. On a hill directly behind the inn is an old-fashioned, steepled church where many visiting couples are married.

In the main farmhouse are five homey bedrooms furnished with Cindi Ehrgott's lifelong collection of antiques and patchwork quilts. Because Cindi and Alan live in another house nearby, guests have free reign of the inn. Two additional suites are in an adjacent carriage house, affording even more privacy. Behind the inn, a garden gazebo overlooks a natural pond with ducks, birds, and bullfrogs. Apparently, a former owner of this farmhouse was a connoisseur of frogs legs, so he filled the pond with frogs. Their descendants are still croaking away.

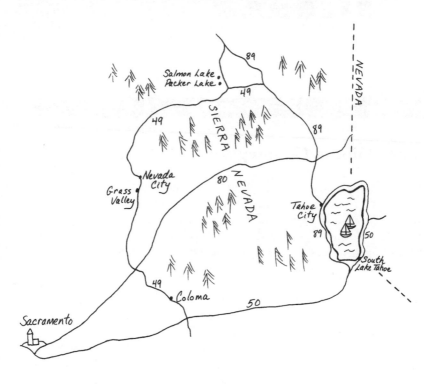

NORTHERN SIERRAS

89

NEVADA

Salmon Lake
Packer Lake

49

SIERRA

49

89

Nevada
City

80

NEVADA

Grass
Valley

Tahoe
City

89

50

South
Lake Tahoe

49

Coloma

50

Sacramento

THE COLOMA COUNTRY INN

Telephone: **(916) 622-6919**
Address: **345 High Street, P.O. Box 502, Coloma 95613**
Rates: **$89 to $99, including full breakfast**
Directions: **in Coloma, on the corner of Church and High Streets.**

GRASS VALLEY

Swan-Levine House

Artists and art lovers will find haven at the Swan-Levine House in Grass Valley. The home's carriage house has been converted into a printmaking studio, complete with etching press and stones. For a small fee, guests can learn how to make monotypes, etchings, and lithographs. The top floor of the main house is a matting and framing studio, also for the guests' use.

Built in 1880, the house was first a private home and then a hospital. For the last two decades it has been run as an inn by artists Howard Levine and Margaret Warner Swan. They have filled the walls of their happily cluttered Queen Anne home with their own artwork, the paintings of other artists, and an amusing collection of memorabilia reflecting the inn's history. The former surgery room, with octagonal white floor tiles, has been turned into a guest room of hot-pink walls and white wicker. They kept the old scrub-up sinks in the bathroom and decorated them with an array of vintage bed pans and hospital paraphernalia. Another room, called the Apartment, was once the former recovery ward. Sporting funky fifties decor, this room has an old wooden wheelchair in the corner. In the adjoining TV room is a fifties television set that Margaret plans to restore.

The spirit of creativity here is contagious and has brought a devoted following of interesting guests for twenty years. Howard and Margaret's children grew up in the house and are now artists themselves. (One son dances with the American Ballet Theatre.) Margaret, an established printmaker, loves demonstrating the process of etching to anyone who is interested.

SWAN-LEVINE HOUSE

Telephone: **(916) 272-1873**
Address: **328 South Church Street, Grass Valley 95945**
Rates: **$55 to $85, including breakfast**
Directions: **From Highway 49, exit at downtown Grass Valley and follow Main Street to Church Street, where you'll turn left.**

LAKE TAHOE

Fantasy Inn

Only a few of the mediocre motels and hotels on the California side of South Lake Tahoe are above the norm in quality. And of those few, I could find only one that was truly exciting—the Fantasy Inn. The alpine exterior looks fresh and new. The sign says "Romantic adult hotel."

It turned out to be the sexiest hotel I've ever seen. Sexy, but also luxurious and sophisticated.

Every room at the Fantasy Inn features mirrored ceilings and walls, romantic lighting (the soft lights turn on and off gradually), an oversized spa with an adjacent open shower for two (with his-and-her shower heads), surround-sound stereo, and a swiveling ceiling television with adult channels. The beds range from round to heart-shaped to waveless waterbeds. Thirteen of the fifty-plus rooms have larger spas and exotic themes with names such as Arabian Nights, Antony and Cleopatra, Marie Antoinette, and Tropical Treehouse. There are also several bigger deluxe theme suites with huge sunken, mosaic-tiled spas, fireplaces, and refrigerators.

The theme suites are a visual extravaganza. For me, the most memorable is Caesar's Indulgence, which features a zebra-patterned carpet, fireplace, seven-foot black marble Jacuzzi tub, and sleek, masculine decor. I also liked the Roman Suite for its round bed, sunken nine-foot spa, Roman columns, and sensuous mural depicting a castle courtyard scene. Antony and Cleopatra is similar, with a tiger carpet and round bed covered in black silk. Romeo and Juliet is a romantic, more innocent favorite for the

The Fantasy Inn, including its Roman Suite, is luxurious, sophisticated, and sexy.

just-married, with its round, white bed, soft pastel furnishings, nine-foot sunken spa, and wall mural of the famous doomed couple. The Graceland Suite, a tribute to Elvis (guitar-shaped coffee table and red, heart-shaped spa) is one I could live without. And the Rainforest Suite, with its jungle theme, is a tad too busy. But overall, every room has something fun to offer.

With its own chapel and in-house wedding coordinator, the Fantasy Inn does a brisk business in weddings. If you book the deluxe fantasy wedding package, you can plan a theme wedding, with appropriate costumes, decor, music, and ceremonial customs.

This hotel is not for the faint of heart. It's playful—no, make that brazenly seductive—but completely tasteful and upscale.

FANTASY INN

Telephone: **(800) 367-7736; (916) 541-6666**
Address: **3696 Lake Tahoe Boulevard, South Lake Tahoe 96150**
Rates: **$110 to $250; ask about their various packages**
Directions: **in South Lake Tahoe, on US-50 (Lake Tahoe Boulevard).**

The Cottage Inn

Of the many cottages and cabins I visited around the western shore of Lake Tahoe, the Cottage Inn is by far the most charming, inside and out. A collection of crisp guest cottages are gathered around a soft central lawn of pines, with hammocks suspended between the trees. In the morning, you can sink into one of the bent willow chairs in the friendly main lodge for a hearty country breakfast. The lake and private beach are just a short stroll through the trees. A Scandinavian sauna is also on the premises

The remodeled, knotty-pine-paneled thirties cottages have a fresh country look. Each cottage has a slightly different theme, but they're all equipped with stone fireplaces, televisions, and VCRs. Romantic Hideaway is especially appealing, with its two-story fireplace, natural rock Jacuzzi, and waterfall. Bird Nest has a spiral staircase built out of undulating pine logs and bent willow that leads to an elevated bird's nest bedroom. The Stagecoach Stop is a step into the Old West, with a steer horn over the fireplace. There's the Old Fishin' Hole, with a fish-patterned bedspread and fishing net curtains; and even a couple of hunting-theme rooms decorated with guns, ducks, deer heads, and a chandelier made from antlers. Guns aren't my cup of tea, but perhaps NRA enthusiasts would just love this.

THE COTTAGE INN

Telephone: (800) 581-4073; (916) 581-4073; fax (916) 581-0226
Address: 1690 West Lake Boulevard, P.O. Box 66, Tahoe City 96145
Rates: $100 to $140, including full breakfast and afternoon wine
Directions: on SR-89, two miles south of Tahoe City.

River Ranch Lodge

If you're looking for a great place to stop for lunch on your way to or from Lake Tahoe, River Ranch Lodge beckons. The outdoor deck hangs right over the Big Bend of picturesque Truckee River. Always a popular watering hole, this informal lodge has been open off and on for more than a hundred years. The guest rooms are clean, decent, and unmemorable except for the few that have balconies overlooking the rapids.

RIVER RANCH LODGE

Telephone: **(800) 535-9900; (916) 583-4264**
Address: **P.O. Box 197, Tahoe City 96145**
Rates: **$39 to $115**
Directions: **on SR-89 and Alpine Meadows Road, west of Tahoe City.**

NEVADA CITY

Red Castle Inn

Here's my favorite place to stay in the Gold Country. The Red Castle Inn has real character and a sense of history few historic bed and breakfasts are able to capture.

Innkeepers Mary Louise and Conley Weaver have layered their inn with unusual Victorian heirlooms, rich fabrics, original works of art, and their own whimsical touches. The place is both historically authentic and charmingly eccentric. In every guest room, for instance, you'll find a vase of peacock feathers (very popular in Victorian times) instead of flowers; the base of the hallway lamp is made from an old-fashioned dressmaking form; my Kleenex box was housed in a vintage fishing tackle basket; and the one telephone at the inn is a turn-of-the-century model.

One of only two Gothic Revival brick buildings on the West Coast, the 1860 inn resembles a gingerbread house with its white icicle wood trim. Each of the four stories has its own verandah or balcony hung with patriotic bunting in the summer. Built on Prospect Hill above Nevada City, "the Castle," as locals called it, used to stand out for miles around. However, the forest has grown so thick around the inn, the town is barely visible from the topmost balcony. On Saturday mornings, you can board a horse-drawn carriage and descend into Nevada City for a tour of the historic district.

In their efforts to preserve another sense of time and place, the Weavers have remained delightfully impervious to the trends of other bed and breakfasts. There are no telephones, no televisions, and no Jacuzzi tubs in the rooms. And you won't find any dried-out blueberry muffins here—Mary Louise has a pastry chef who bakes the most divine, melt-in-your-mouth creations for breakfast and tea. The menu always includes an heirloom recipe or historic culinary treat.

During afternoon tea, Mark Twain and Lola Montez look-alikes often make impromptu appearances and carry on nineteenth-century conversations with the guests. Lola might even do a toned-down version of her famous spider dance for you.

A ghostly spirit named Laura Jean might make another impromptu appearance. A former young governess of the house, she is said to be a soothing presence. Even Conley, the owner, saw her once. Although I've never encountered any spirits myself, I can't think of a more comforting place to have such an experience than at the Red Castle Inn.

RED CASTLE INN

Telephone: **(916) 265-5135**
Address: **109 Prospect Street, Nevada City 95959**
Rates: **$100 to $125, including full breakfast and afternoon tea**
Directions: **From Highway 49 north, exit at Sacramento Street in Nevada City; take a right turn on Adams Street and an immediate left fork on Prospect Street.**

Flume's End

Ever try your hand at gold panning? Flume's End hovers right over Gold Run Creek, where gold is still found on occasion. The innkeepers will even provide the gold pan. The historic flume beside the inn is no longer in use, but it was originally seventeen miles long.

With its beautiful country setting in Nevada City, the inn is terraced down a steep hillside to a natural waterfall and creek that meanders through a three-acre tunnel of trees. A few chairs are ideally positioned on a narrow promontory next to the waterfall and over the creek. One guest room, Creekside, is situated right over the falls.

FLUME'S END

Telephone: **(916) 265-9665**
Address: **317 South Pine Street, Nevada City 95959**
Rates: **$75 to $135, including full breakfast**
Directions: **From SR-49, exit at Broad Street in Nevada City; turn left on Pine Street and cross the narrow bridge.**

LITTLE NOVELTY: Each of the six guest rooms at the **Downey House** in Nevada City comes with its own fish tank. The beds of this East-lake-style Victorian bed and breakfast are decorated with fish pillows, too. For more information, call the Downey House at (800) 258-2815 or (916) 265-2815.

The Expanding Light

A wonderful retreat that is part of Ananda (a cooperative village founded by a disciple of Paramhansa Yogananda), the Expanding Light is about a half-hour north of Nevada City. Situated on a forested hilltop, the vast grounds include miles of walking paths among the pine trees. Accommodations consist of individual cabins with a communal bathhouse, plus double rooms with shared bath in the Serenity House—a cheery building which is so spotless, you remove your shoes at the front door before entering.

Although the main focus at the Expanding Light is meditation and yoga, you don't have to participate in the classes in order to stay here. If you are looking for a quiet, unstructured experience, ask for the Personal Retreat. You have the option of joining in the activities—twice-daily yoga and meditation, classes and outings, and personal spiritual counseling—as much or as little as you want. It's a friendly place where people from any spiritual background would feel comfortable. (They even have Elderhostel programs here.) Before meditation, the group leaders start with a prayer to their guru, but they don't pressure you to join in.

Of all the retreats I visited in California, my first two choices would be Esalen or the Expanding Light. I tend to favor yoga-oriented retreats, but I also like ones that leave you free to do your own thing. At the Expanding Light, you can enjoy many of the amenities found at a pricey spa—nature trails, yoga classes, massages, meditation, and healthy vegetarian food—at a fraction of the cost. A Personal Retreat week at the Expanding Light costs around five hundred dollars (even less for a shared room); a week at the Golden Door, by the way, is over four thousand dollars.

THE EXPANDING LIGHT

Telephone: **(800) 346-5350**
Address: **14618 Tyler Foote Road, Nevada City 95959**
Rates: **$62 per person for a shared room, including all meals, classes, and activities; $85 per person for a private room**
Directions: **From Highway 49 north (eleven miles north of Nevada City), turn right on Tyler Foote Road (at the sign for Malakoff Diggins State Park). After five miles, turn left at the Ananda Village sign and left again at the next intersection.**

PACKER LAKE

Packer Lake Lodge

Every cabin comes with its own rowboat at Packer Lake Lodge. The simple, formica-floored cabins are scattered in various spots around remote Packer Lake. Those farthest from the lake have private baths and kitchens; those closest to the lake share two communal baths called Bullpen and Cowshed.

Dream House has the most idyllic setting I've ever seen for a lakeside cabin. Built of logs, it's romantically nestled among the trees right at the water's edge, with a rowboat pulled onto the shore directly in front. It also has a little sun deck and picnic table. The only hitches—no private bath and no kitchen. Bring a flashlight for those midnight trips to the Cowshed.

PACKER LAKE LODGE

Telephone: **(916) 862-1221 May to November; (415) 921-5943 November to May; closed between snows**
Reservations: **P.O. Box 237, Sierra City 96125 (in season); 2245 Beach Street, Apartment 2, San Francisco 94123 (off season)**
Rates: **$54 to $110, including one rowboat**
Directions: **From Highway 49, nine miles north of Sierra City, head north on Gold Lake Road; after four and one-half miles, turn left on Sardine Lake Road and follow signs to Packer Lake.**

SACRAMENTO

The *Delta King*

From 1927 to 1940, the *Delta King* paddled the San Francisco-to-Sacramento pleasure route with its sister ship, the *Delta Queen*. During World War II, the riverboat served as troop barracks on the San Francisco Bay. In the 1980s, the *Delta King* sank into the bay and remained immersed up to its fourth deck for fifteen months until it was finally dredged up.

Today, the renovated *Delta King* is permanently moored in Old Sacramento as the only stern-wheeler lodging in California. Its forty-three guest rooms have brass or rattan beds, televisions tucked away in armoires, and other modern conveniences. They're fine, if not memorable. More impressive is the Captain's Quarters, a three-room penthouse suite in the original wheelhouse. It has its own private deck with views of the Sacramento River and a catwalk leading to the massive wheel. A brass sign at the wheel reads, "The captain's word is law."

The riverboat has a restaurant, lounge, and saloon that faces to the stern. On occasion, live productions are held in the boat's theater.

A great perk of the *Delta King* (photo, page 184) is having Old Town right outside your cabin door. It's a delightful historic district of old-fashioned shops, museums, and restaurants.

THE *DELTA KING*

Telephone: **(800) 825-KING; (916) 444-KING**
Address: **1000 Front Street, Old Sacramento 95814**
Rates: **$89 to $400, including continental breakfast**
Directions: **From I-5 in central Sacramento, follow the signs to Old Sacramento. *Delta King* is on the riverfront.**

The Sacramento Hostel

As far as hostels go, the Sacramento Hostel is one of the most elegant in California. Housed in a grand old Victorian, the building is full of ornate detailing—carved oak staircase, pillars, frescoed

The Delta King *once paddled the San Francisco-to-Sacramento pleasure route. (See page 183.)*

ceilings, tiled fireplaces, and a glass skylight. Like other hostels in the state, this one is closed during the day and the cleaning responsibilities are shared. People of all ages are welcome in the dormitory rooms.

Situated in a relatively decent part of the city, the Sacramento Hostel is only six blocks from the State Capitol and Old Sacramento. When I was there, people were coming from the farmer's market at the nearby Downtown Plaza, their arms full of produce.

THE SACRAMENTO HOSTEL

Telephone: **(916) 443-1691**
Address: **900 H Street, Sacramento 95814**
Rates: **$10 to $12 per person**
Directions: **From I-5 south, exit at J Street; turn left on Eighth Street and right on H Street.**

Amber House

If you have a weakness for luxurious bathrooms, you'll be fond of the Amber House in Sacramento. Nearly every one of the nine guest rooms in this side-by-side pair of houses has a sybaritic bathroom, with a marble whirlpool tub for two, luxury soaps, and thick, white terry robes. My favorite is the Van Gogh Room (see page 186): From the bedroom, wide French doors open to a solarium-like bathroom with a black-and-white-checked marble floor, mint green walls, and windows that run to the ceiling. The bathroom is large enough to easily hold a heart-shaped whirlpool tub for two and white wicker chaise longue. Take note, however, there is a shade you can pull over the windows for privacy. I didn't discover this until I was checking out the next day—after I had already spent an inordinate amount of time lolling about in the tub, assuming the windows were tinted on the outside. The innkeeper assured me the neighbors across the alley are used to seeing unclothed guests by now, but he might have just been trying to placate my embarrassment.

AMBER HOUSE

Telephone: **(800) 755-6526; (916) 444-8085; fax (916) 552-6529**
Address: **1315 Twenty-second Street, Sacramento 95816**
Rates: **$89 to $139, single occupancy; $99 to $199, double occupancy, including full breakfast**
Directions: **on Twenty-second Street, between Capitol Avenue and N Street.**

SALMON LAKE

Salmon Lake Lodge

You can't find a location much more secluded than Salmon Lake Lodge. To reach this twenties family resort, you have to hike around the lake for twenty minutes, or phone for the lodge's barge to pick you up. Accommodations consist of tent cabins (with wood floors and walls, and canvas roof) and rustic cabins on the hillside, ridge, and lake. Each cabin is equipped with an electric stove, small refrigerator, and barbecue. (The ridge cabins have fully equipped kitchens.) You bring your own bedding, towels, cooking utensils, and food.

Amber House's Van Gogh Room offers one of the many trademark luxury baths at the inn. (See pages 184–185.)

Situated at 6,500 feet in a remote northeast corner of the Sierras, sparkling Salmon Lake is surrounded by rocky, forested foothills. The lodge guests have free use of fishing boats, small sailboats, canoes, and kayaks. Each week during the summer, the lodge caters a barbecue on a little island in the middle of the lake. You can literally paddle out to the island for your dinner.

SALMON LAKE LODGE

Telephone: **(916) 842-3108**
Reservations: **Box 121, Sierra City 96125**
Rates: **$400 to $900 per week, including use of boats**
Directions: **From Highway 49, nine miles northwest of Sierra City, head north on Gold Lake Road; turn left at the sign for Salmon Lake.**

AMADOR CITY

Imperial Hotel

The guest rooms at the Imperial Hotel have a beguiling sense of whimsy that set it apart from other Gold Country hotels. In Room Three, for example, the armoire is painted to look like there are clothes spilling out from the doors. Room Two also has a trompe l'oeil armoire, while Room Five features a tall, fancifully painted headboard. Room Six is a total departure from the others, with its art deco appointments.

These innovative touches are coupled with reminders of the hotel's nineteenth-century history—exposed brick walls, antique furnishings, and a cozy, old-fashioned bar. But it has none of the tiredness that often accompanies older hotels. There's a fresh fragrance in the air. The aromas emanating from the dining room are heavenly. Extra niceties such as bath salts, hair dryers, and heated towel bars are provided in the pristine white bathrooms. Altogether, the Imperial Hotel is an inviting little gem.

IMPERIAL HOTEL

Telephone: **(800) 242-5594; (209) 267-9172**
Address: **P.O. Box 195, Amador City 95601**
Rates: **$75 to $90, including continental breakfast**
Directions: **on SR-49, in Amador City.**

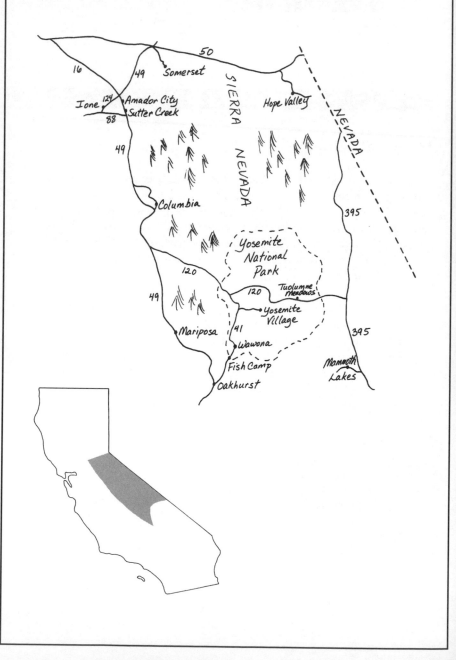

COLUMBIA

City Hotel and
Fallon Hotel

Considered the best-preserved gold-mining town in California, Columbia is a living museum and state historic park. Most of the day, only horse-drawn carriages are allowed on the main street where you'll find businesses carrying on much as they did in the mid-1800s. The *Columbia Gazette,* still in operation, is housed in a replica of its 1855 office. There's also a working blacksmith's shop, pharmacy, and saloon. At the mining supply store you can learn how to pan for gold. Many of the shopkeepers are authentically costumed.

In the heart of town is the City Hotel, which has been providing rooms to wayfarers for more than 130 years. Based around a central parlor, its second-floor guest rooms are largely unchanged from Victorian times except for a few modern conveniences. They're small and simple, with high ceilings, wood floors, period furnishings, and some elaborately carved beds. Showers are down the hall.

Another novel aspect of the City Hotel is that most of the staff are students in the hospitality management program at Columbia College. Though some are gaining work experience in hotel management, the majority are working as food service trainees in the hotel's dining room. With this in mind, one would naturally expect rather spotty consistency. On the contrary—the City Hotel's dining room has an excellent reputation. During the first two weeks at Christmas, a Victorian Christmas feast is held every night. The black-tie affair is hosted by a man who claims to be Mr. George Morgan, original founder of the 1856 hotel. Some of his cronies make special appearances throughout the night, adding a bit of music and entertainment to the festivities.

Down the street and also within the park is their sister hotel, the Fallon Hotel, home of the Columbia Actors Repertory. Their year-round theater productions, held in the hotel's historic theater, can be booked as part of a package with either the Fallon or City Hotel.

I had heard that Columbia could be a real zoo of tourists and traffic. But when I visited the town on a September weekday, I had the whole place to myself. Walking through an almost deserted gold town made the living history experience all the more authentic.

CITY HOTEL

Telephone: **(209) 532-1479**
Address: **P.O. Box 1870, Columbia 95310**
Rates: **$70 to $95, including continental breakfast**
Directions: **in downtown Columbia.**

FALLON HOTEL

Telephone: **(209) 532-1470**
Address: **P.O. Box 1870, Columbia 95310**
Rates: **$55 to $95, including continental breakfast**
Directions: **on the south side of downtown Columbia.**

CROWLEY LAKE

Rainbow Tarns

Traveling with your horse? At Rainbow Tarns, you *and* your horse are welcome. Situated just off US-395 at seven thousand feet above sea level, this rustic twenties log house nestles against a hillside of dramatic boulders. On the front porch, handmade leather rockers overlook a soft green lawn, shimmering aspens, and several fish-filled creeks spilling into one another. The log living room has high beamed ceilings, a large rock fireplace, and a deer's head mounted above the mantel. Out back is a chicken coop (the source of eggs for breakfast) and horse stables, with a wide grazing field beyond. This is a happy, Old West kind of place—a delightful stopover on your way up the eastern Sierras.

RAINBOW TARNS

Telephone: **(619) 935-4556**
Address: **Route 1, Box 1097, Crowley Lake 93546**
Rates: **$95 to $125, including full breakfast and afternoon refreshments**
Directions: **twenty-four miles north of Bishop; from US-395 (at the summit), turn left at the sign for Tom's Place; make an immediate right on Crowley Lake Road, then right at Rainbow Tarns Road.**

FISH CAMP

The Narrow Gauge Inn

The Narrow Gauge Inn is named in honor of the adjacent Yosemite Mountain Sugar Pine Railroad, which offers four-mile scenic narrow-gauge rail excursions on vintage, steam-powered locomotives and trolley-like railcars. Situated just outside Yosemite's southern border, the historic rail route passes through some of the prettiest scenery in the Sierra National Forest. On Saturday evenings from May to October, the steam train excursion is high-lighted by a steak barbecue dinner and music around a campfire.

The motor inn not only makes an ideal stopover for rail enthusiasts, but it's also a quiet place, landscaped with colorful flowers and fragrant incense cedar trees. There is a small swimming pool and hot tub, a dining hall, and the Buffalo Bar. The inn houses its own shiny, vintage fire engine—one that really works.

THE NARROW GAUGE INN

Telephone: **(209) 683-7720**
Address: **48571 Highway 41, Fish Camp 93623; closed in winter**
Rates: **$85 to $130**
Directions: **on SR-41, four miles south of Yosemite Park border.**

HOPE VALLEY

Sorensen's

An adorable resort, Sorensen's is isolated in a wide alpine valley south of Lake Tahoe. A cluster of cheery cabins are nestled against the pine-covered hill, offering an interesting range of accommodations.

To begin with, there's the Norway House, built in Norway as a replica of a thirteenth-century building. The two-story, intricately carved, sod-roof cabin was imported log by log from Norway. Two of the other larger cabins—Saint Nick's and the

The Norway House at Sorenson's is a replica of a thirteenth-century building.

Chapel—were rescued from the now defunct Santa's Village near Santa Cruz. Both look every bit the quintessential Christmas cottage. Saint Nick's is a fanciful rendition of Santa's House—an A-frame log cabin with red- and green-trimmed interior and a spiral staircase that leads up to the bedroom. The Chapel, an old-fashioned log cabin, is trimmed in white icicles and features hand-hewn doorways, a rock hearth, and circular staircase up to the bedroom loft.

There are all kinds of cabins here—big, small, log, redwood, old, and new. Johan's, for instance, is so tiny the bed is raised off the floor for extra storage space underneath. Another cabin is a converted dance hall. Piñon (with its clawfoot tub and bubble bath) and Waterfir (with its natural rock hearth) are two romantic favorites despite their small size. From Rock Creek you can hear the babbling brook outside.

Operated by John and Patty Brissenden, the twenties resort has a friendly, family atmosphere, with inviting hammocks and Adirondack chairs under the pine and aspen trees. During the winter, cross-country skiers can attempt the resort's ten kilometers of groomed trails and ninety kilometers of ungroomed trails. In the summer, they offer river rafting, birding excursions, banjo instruction, wildflower walks, historic tours of the Emigrant Trail, astronomy classes, and fly-fishing classes in the resort's pond. If you snag that special trout, they'll cook it for you in the country-style cafe.

SORENSEN'S

Telephone: **(800) 423-9949; (916) 694-2203**
Address: **14255 Highway 88, Hope Valley 96120**
Rates: **$55 to $225; some rates include breakfast**
Directions: **just east of SR-88/89 junction, twenty-eight miles south of Lake Tahoe.**

IONE

The Heirloom

Those looking for a touch of the South right here in California will find it at the Heirloom, a Greek Revival mansion in the Sierra foothills. Built in 1863 by a settler from Virginia, the red brick mansion is graced by white columns and cooled by century-old magnolia trees. Innkeepers Patricia Cross and Melisande Hubbs have filled the home with a comfortable blend of their family heirlooms. Gracious women, they both fit perfectly into these lovely surroundings, often greeting their guests in matching, old-fashioned dresses.

Down the gravel driveway and in complete contrast to this delicate mansion is the newly built Adobe Cottage—an ecological experiment of the innkeepers. The sixteen-inch thick walls are built of rammed earth. The roof is sod, with a sprinkler system added for extra insulation. When the grass gets too high on the roof, they actually take a mower to it. Inside, the two guest rooms are decorated in early American and early California styles, with wood-burning stoves and local hardwoods.

THE HEIRLOOM

Telephone: **(209) 274-4468**
Address: **214 Shakeley Lane, P.O. Box 322, Ione 95640**
Rates: **$55 to $97, including full breakfast**
Directions: **east of Highway 49, midway between Lake Tahoe and Yosemite; in Ione, turn left on Main Street, right on Preston, and left on Shakeley Lane.**

MAMMOTH LAKES

Tamarack Lodge Resort

As beautiful as the scenery is, Mammoth Lakes is lacking when it comes to lodgings with character. Unlike other ski towns that are filled with charming inns and hotels (Aspen and Park City), Mammoth is just a maze of condos, motels, and minimalls that all look the same. This is a no-frills town for hardcore skiers.

If you drive a few miles beyond Mammoth, however, you'll find a delightful exception at the Tamarack Lodge Resort. Built in 1924, this classic old lodge and its rustic cabins overlook the sparkling waters of Twin Lakes. Adjacent to the lodge is a cross-country ski center offering a wonderland of quiet winter trails. Throughout the summer, trout fishermen, women, and kids are lined along the tranquil banks of the lake while a waterfall cascades in the distance.

The lodge's lounge has a comforting feel with a big stone fireplace and the cat asleep on the sofa. I also like the lace-curtain atmosphere of the cute, somewhat overpriced restaurant down the hall. The only weakness of this lodge is the drab interior of each bedroom and cabin, with mottled brown carpeting and thin wood paneling. All cabins are equipped with full kitchens; a few have fireplaces.

Close to the lodge, crossing the bridge between Twin Lakes, you'll find an outdoor chapel hidden in the woods. With the breeze wafting through the pine trees, sunlight shimmering on the lakes, and the mountains all around you, this nature-at-its-best setting makes a great location for ceremonies, especially weddings.

TAMARACK LODGE RESORT

Telephone: **(800) 237-6879; (619) 934-2442**
Address: **P.O. Box 69, Mammoth Lakes 93546**
Rates: **$45 to $360**
Directions: **two and one-half miles up Lake Mary Road from Mammoth Lakes.**

Mammoth Mountain Inn

Most skiers are familiar with Mammoth Mountain Inn because it's right across the street from the ski area's main lodge. A big A-frame, the hotel has two hundred-plus rooms and predictable, contemporary lodge decor. At the end of ski season, I assumed the hotel rolled up its carpets until the next snow. That's why I was surprised to drive up during the summer and find its parking lot full of cars and bustling activity. A massive granite boulder had been moved to the front lawn, and people of all ages were struggling to the top with mountain-climbing gear.

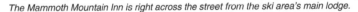

The Mammoth Mountain Inn is right across the street from the ski area's main lodge.

The Mammoth Mountain Inn offers a whole menu of summer adventure packages, including kayaking, golf, fishing, and mountain biking. Their most unique package is a three-part course in adventure—with challenge ropes, orienteering, and wall climbing. The ropes course consists of a series of outdoor obstacles using ropes and cables. The orienteering course teaches how to use a map and compass for land navigation. And the thirty-foot climbing wall is set up for climbers of all ages and abilities. Judging by the number of people gathered around the rock, it is enormously popular.

MAMMOTH MOUNTAIN INN

Telephone:	**(800) 228-4947; (619) 934-2581**
Address:	**P.O. Box 353, Mammoth Lakes 93546**
Rates:	**$85 to $175; inquire about packages**
Directions:	**on Minaret Road, across from Mammoth ski area's main lodge.**

MARIPOSA

LITTLE NOVELTY: Whenever people telephone the **Meadow Creek Ranch,** they usually say, "We want the chicken coop." Yes, the chicken coop of this Lincoln-era ranch and former stagecoach stop has been charmingly converted into a country-style guest cottage, complete with flower boxes, an Austrian bed, and clawfoot tub. The chickens, however, have since moved on to that great coop in the sky. For more information, call (209) 966-3843.

OAKHURST

Château du Sureau

"We don't do eggs and bacon here," Erna Kubin-Clanin said as she led me past the koi pond of her luxurious little château. From the moment I pulled up to the electronic gate and a voice on the

Your next move should be an excursion to Château du Sureau.

intercom said, *"Bonjour, Château du Sureau,"* I already knew this wasn't a bacon-and-eggs kind of place. *C'est très élégant.*

Only five years old, Château du Sureau is handcrafted in the traditional Provençal style with a red tile roof and stone turret. Inside, the whitewashed walls are accented by dark wood beams, and the terra cotta floors are covered with Oriental carpets. Tapestries and old etchings of Lyons and St. Germain hang on the walls. The adjacent restaurant, Erna's Elderberry House, is renowned for its fabulous six-course dinners. You can't get any closer to France in all of California. In the tradition of most French castles, the Château even has its own tiny chapel (with three pews) where proposals and weddings take place.

Viennese-born Erna runs a tight ship at the Château. We passed a room where several young men were discreetly cleaning, and they were all formally dressed in black pants, white shirts, and bow ties. An obvious perfectionist, Erna has mapped out every tasteful detail, sparing no expense on quality. Silky soft, five-hundred-thread-count sheets dress the beds, and the evening turndown is artfully performed. Every guest room offers a fireplace, built-in stereo system with classical CDs, soaking tub, old-fashioned telephone, and complimentary treats.

Guests are invited to tinkle the keys of the grand piano which sits within the turret of the Château's formal living room. It's an exquisite space, with soft murals on the walls and tapestried chairs before the hearth. Through the mullioned windows, you can look out to the surrounding pines and oaks. Down the footpath you'll come upon another surprise—an outdoor chess game with chessmen standing several feet high.

One would expect to find a place this grand in the wine country, perhaps, but not in the down-home Sierra foothills. The Château dominates the hill above Oakhurst—gateway to the Gold Country and Yosemite—in complete contrast to the suburban town. But when viewed from this tranquil spot, the daily routine of the suburbs seems quite distant.

CHÂTEAU DU SUREAU

Telephone:	**(209) 683-6860; fax (209) 683-0800**
Address:	**48688 Victoria Lane, P.O. Box 577, Oakhurst 93644**
Rates:	**$310 to $400, including full breakfast**
Directions:	**off SR-41, just south of SR-49; tours by appointment only.**

SOMERSET

Fitzpatrick Winery & Lodge

Wine lovers will delight in the Fitzpatrick Winery & Lodge, a handcrafted log lodge situated high above the Sierra foothills. "Winekeepers" Brian and Diana Fitzpatrick offer weekend wine tasting and year-round bed and breakfast accommodations.

Operating since 1980, Brian and Diana were the first to open a winery in this remote pocket of the Sierras. Now there are seven wineries within a three-mile radius. Much of the Fitzpatrick wine is made from organically grown grapes, using only a minuscule amount of sulfites. On weekends, you can sample their products and enjoy a ploughman's lunch in the tasting room.

Of the four guest rooms, the Log Suite is the largest, with massive log walls and overhead viga ceilings. Like the rest of the lodge, it's furnished in a loose, informal manner. And although the hospitality is indisputable, the winery takes precedence over the lodgings. Whether you stay here or not, at least come to sample the wine and the view—especially in June, when the Fairplay Wine Festival takes place

FITZPATRICK WINERY & LODGE

Telephone:	**(800) 245-9166; (209) 620-3248; fax (209) 620-6838**
Address:	**7740 Fairplay Road, Somerset 95684**
Rates:	**$69 to $99, including breakfast and wine tasting**
Directions:	**From Mount Aukum Road, six miles southeast of Somerset, turn left on Fairplay Road (at Gray's Market) and proceed for several miles.**

SUTTER CREEK

Sutter Creek Inn

In 1966 Sutter Creek Inn became one of the state's first bed and breakfasts to open. Original owner Jane Way is now seventy-something, but she certainly doesn't look it. Full of spirit and warmth, Jane has always been adamant about keeping her prices affordable. Her tree-shaded grounds contain a handsome New England-style house and eighteen somewhat-dated guest rooms in various historic outbuildings. A room in the restored woodshed or wash house starts at only fifty dollars with a full breakfast—a good rate for a California bed and breakfast.

Sutter Creek Inn offers two novelties I've never encountered—swinging beds and handwriting analysis. The mattresses in four of the guest rooms are suspended by chains from the ceiling. They can be stabilized, but most guests prefer to leave them swinging. If you can't get one of these rooms, there are plenty of hammocks available under the grape arbors.

By appointment, Jane will also analyze your handwriting, with a little surprise thrown in at the end. These slight eccentricities, the decent rates, and peaceful ambiance of the inn have brought Jane a loyal following of return guests for three decades.

SUTTER CREEK INN

Telephone: **(209) 267-5606**
Address: **75 Main Street, P.O. Box 385, Sutter Creek 95685**
Rates: **$50 to $135, including full breakfast**
Directions: **on Highway 49, in downtown Sutter Creek.**

> **LITTLE NOVELTY:** The Hanford House in Sutter Creek has what the innkeepers fondly call their "Graffiti Room"—the white walls and ceilings of the dining room are covered in comments written by guests. If you want to add to it, grab a ladder and search for a little blank corner. But be forewarned: If you write outside the border of the dining room, you're handed a brush and required to paint one of the guest rooms. For more information, call (800) 871-5839 or (209) 267-0747.

WAWONA

Wawona Hotel

The Wawona Hotel looks like a graceful gathering of southern belles dressed all in white, reclined against a luxuriant slope of grass. The Victorian-style main building, with its verandah of white wicker rockers, would be a perfect spot for sipping mint juleps. Delicate strands of ivy creep up the sides of cottages and guest annexes. White Adirondack chairs are arranged under the trees by the swimming pool, while a fountain gurgles on the front lawn. A lovely nine-hole golf course meanders through the surrounding forested hills.

If you don't mind staying twenty-five miles from Yosemite Village, the Wawona Hotel makes a wonderful base for exploring the national park. It's less than half the price of the Ahwahnee and has almost as much character—although it's completely different in style. It is one of California's oldest mountain resort hotels. (The first cottage was built in 1876.) Moore Cottage, behind the main building, is the prettiest of the guest quarters. Since the hotel is part of Yosemite's park service, you can request a particular room, but nothing is guaranteed.

WAWONA HOTEL

Telephone: **(209) 252-4848**
Reservations: **write to Yosemite Reservations, 5410 East Home Avenue, Fresno 93727**
Rates: **$68.25 to $91.35**
Directions: **in Wawona, on SR-41**

YOSEMITE NATIONAL PARK

Tuolumne Meadows Lodge

Structurally, all of the tent cabins in Yosemite National Park are much the same. Whether you stay at Curry Village, White Wolf Lodge, or Tuolumne Meadows Lodge, your tent cabin will have a wood or concrete floor and white canvas walls. All come equipped with cot-like beds (some doubles and some twins), linens, blankets, towels for the community bathrooms, a mirror, single light bulb, and shelf for your things. Neither cooking facilities nor heat or electrical outlets are available. (Indeed, any food in your tent cabin is prohibited because of bears.) Meals are taken in a central lodge.

From there, the similarities end. After visiting all three locations, Tuolumne Meadows Lodge ranks a roaring first place. Set at an altitude of 8,600 feet in the beautiful high country of eastern Yosemite (the largest subalpine meadow in the Sierras), it's by far the most atmospheric. Unlike Curry Village, where you're packed together like sardines, the tent cabins at Tuolumne Meadows are spaced comfortably. At Tuolumne Meadows, all is quiet except for the sound of the creek rushing by. At Curry Village, we had to stand in line for everything—reservations, food, showers, phones—but there are no lines at Tuolumne Meadows. There are

Tent cabins at Tuolumne Meadows Lodge offer a cozy, back-to-the-basics alternative.

no concession stands or plastic–packed salads; just one simple lodge cafe where cooks will prepare your freshly caught trout.

Even the wildlife seems less aggressive at Tuolumne Meadows. While my girlfriend and I were seated on the steps of our tent cabin at Curry Village (We were trying to get rid of the last of our peanuts, only to find out later that you're not supposed to feed the animals), a squirrel scurried right up her back and into her hair. It happened so fast, I was incredulous until she showed me the muddy little squirrel prints trailing up the back of her blouse.

TUOLUMNE MEADOWS LODGE

    Telephone: **(209) 252-4848; closed in winter**
Reservations: **write to Yosemite Reservations, 5410 East Home Avenue, Fresno 93727**
       Rate: **$41.25**
   Directions: **at Tuolumne Meadows, just south of SR-120.**

The sheer, gray granite Royal Arches make for a spectacular backdrop to the Ahwahnee.

The Ahwahnee

If I could afford it, I would stay at the Ahwahnee on every trip to Yosemite. Heck, if I could afford it, I would live there. This grand old hotel is like Yosemite itself—it has to be seen.

Built of granite and concrete beams stained to look like redwood, the Ahwahnee rises from the valley floor with a patrician serenity, blending in perfectly with the sheer, gray granite backdrop of Royal Arches. The view from the expansive back lawns is spectacular.

The public rooms are equally impressive. In the Great Lounge where afternoon tea is served, the stained-glass windows (designed in the pattern of American Indian logos) rise two stories on either side of the enormous room. The stone fireplaces are so massive you can walk into them. The wood floors, thirties-style sofas, art deco touches, Kilim rugs on the walls (one hundred rugs were purchased for the hotel in 1927), and wrought-iron chandeliers all combine marvelously together. And the dining room will simply take your breath away. With its stone walls, high timbered ceilings, tall mullioned windows, and medieval, wrought-iron chandeliers, this massive room looks positively baronial. While we were waiting to be seated at one of the many candlelit tables for dinner, I heard a little girl cry, "It looks like a castle!"

Christmas dinners are enormously popular here. Since its opening in 1927 (except for a few years during World War II when the hotel served as a recuperative center for the war department), the Ahwahnee has held an annual, old-fashioned Bracebridge Dinner—peacock pie, boar's head, and comic entertainment by a court jester—over the course of five nights leading up to Christmas. To secure a seat for the seven-course dinner, you must enter a lottery the first week of December one year in advance. Every year, more than twenty thousand people vie for eighteen hundred seats. The competition is just as fierce at New Year's, too. But it's hard to imagine anything more romantic than spending Christmas at the Ahwahnee, with the whole valley dusted in snow. When it comes to Christmas rituals, the staff goes all out, with storytelling, concerts, the lighting of the yule log, and, of course, the arrival of Santa Claus.

When my friend and I checked into the Ahwahnee and saw how gorgeous it was, we immediately discarded our ambitious afternoon plans of exploring the valley. Instead, we wound up on lounge chairs out by the circular swimming pool, mimosas in hand, drinking in the scenery. We discovered the best way to see Yosemite is from a reclined position—this way, you avoid a stiff neck from looking up so much. And there's no better spot from which to watch the sun set on Half Dome than on the hotel's outdoor terrace.

No matter which side of the hotel your room is on, you'll have an incredible view, especially if you request the fourth, fifth, or sixth floor. (Room 507, one of the most desirable, shares a huge balcony with Room 502 at no extra cost.) We had a room facing Yosemite Falls, the highest falls in the country. In the morning, the falls put on a spectacular undulating rainbow show as the first rays of sun hit. From the other side of the hotel, you can see Glacier Point and Half Dome.

The bedrooms don't have the same thirties ambiance that pervades the hotel, but their views are fantastic. All the luxuries are included—turndown service, terry robes, soaps, and morning coffee in the hallway. If you really want to go for broke, request one of the four suites in the lodge. The Sun Suite, one of the most popular, is on the sixth floor, with a balcony and view of Glacier Point and Half Dome. You can also request one of the twenty-five cottages tucked among the trees behind the hotel. They don't have air conditioning or the views the hotel has, but they are more spacious, with individual patios and a nice sense of privacy.

Although everyone warns you to book the Ahwahnee a year in advance, I was able to get a room for August by calling only two months ahead. I'm not recommending you wait that late—I was stunned when they told me they had an opening—but the receptionist said an average of three out of ten people are able to get reservations just two months in advance.

THE AHWAHNEE

Telephone: **(209) 252-4848**
Reservations: **write to Yosemite Reservations, 5410 East Home Avenue, Fresno 93727**
Rates: **$194.05 to $460**
Directions: **in Yosemite Valley, three-quarters of a mile east of park headquarters.**

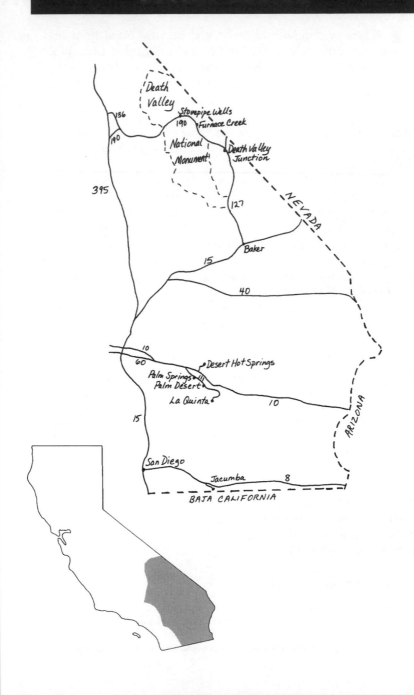

12 DESERT REGION

Two Bunch Palms

Few lodgings guard the privacy of their guests as staunchly as Two Bunch Palms, which is one reason why 80 percent of its clientele are in the entertainment industry. Julia Roberts, Madonna, Goldie Hawn, Mel Gibson, and Bruce Springsteen are just a few of the big-time players who have escaped here for a bit of hedonistic R and R. It's no wonder that the ultimate industry satire, *The Player,* was filmed here. (Remember the scene where Tim Robbins and Greta Scacchi were immersed in mud baths?)

The one hundred-acre spa is built like a veritable fortress (perhaps because it allegedly served as Al Capone's hideout in the old days). No one gains entry without a two-night room reservation. I can vouch for that: I tried to make an appointment for a tour of the resort and was politely refused; I could see it only by booking two full nights. I would love nothing better than to be pampered and pummeled for two whole days at Two Bunch Palms, but my pocketbook protested. When you add the cost of the room, the treatments, and meals, it can easily run into five hundred dollars a day. For Madonna, sure; for a movie executive, maybe; but for a mere mortal like me, this is a special-occasion kind of place.

Nonetheless, Two Bunch Palms should be included here because it offers some unusual treatments along with the usual Swedish massage, shiatsu, and aromatherapy. One of the most intriguing is the Watsu, in which a therapist pulls a floating guest around a private, hot mineral-water pool, rocking and stretching the body. They also offer Jin Shin Do, a gentle, meditative acupressure. Or you can experience a purely intuitive massage called Esoteric. The Native American massage involves a camphor sauna and gentle body brush of fresh eucalyptus, healing oils, and herbal sheet.

Couples can enjoy side-by-side massages in a tropical pagoda overlooking the lake, or the Roman Tub Rejuvenator—a one-hour massage and a lavender Epsom salt bath by candlelight. Then, of course, there are the famous mud baths—green clay warmed by the hot mineral water. If you can still walk after all this, there are private "sun bins," designed for tanning au naturel.

TWO BUNCH PALMS

Telephone: **(800) 472-4334; (619) 329-8791**
Address: **67-425 Two Bunch Palms Trail, Desert Hot Springs 92240**
Rates: **$120 to $570, including continental breakfast**
Directions: **From I-10, exit at Palm Drive; head north to Two Bunch Palms Trail and turn right.**

JACUMBA

Jacumba Hot Springs Spa Lodge and Resort

I first heard about Jacumba Hot Springs from my cousin, who is an L.A. architect. Once a year she and her husband leave their high-stress city jobs and make a four-hour pilgrimage from L.A. to Jacumba (pronounced "Hacoomba"), a tiny little town only six miles from the Mexican border. The motel is run by a German couple named Felix and Lisa Bachmeier. For fifty dollars a night, guests can spend their weekend soaking in the motel's warm, sulfur-spring-fed pool (sometimes accompanied by German swimhause music) and indoor Jacuzzi, breathing the clean desert air, doing absolutely nothing.

Before I made my first pilgrimage to Jacumba, my cousin warned me the rooms were monastic, and the place was "definitely not for the Lexus crowd." When I called for directions, the man on the phone laughed and said, "Jacumba has a population of only four hundred. You can't miss us."

What I found out there in the middle of nowhere was a funky little motel. Built in the ubiquitous U-shape around the pool, the rooms are somewhat stale and completely lacking in charm, but functional. The swimming pool area is quite pleasant, with shade trees, climbing roses, and singing birds. As I floated around in the sulfury pool, unwinding from the long drive, I realized this place was so utterly and happily tacky, there was something rather endearing about it. It's completely unspoiled by any pretensions.

Energetic, Bavarian-born Felix is much in evidence about the grounds, behind the desk, in the motel's bar (where all the "Southern Exposure"-type local characters gather at night), and in the restaurant, which features plain, stick-to-your-ribs German food. When a lodge is German-owned, no matter how remote, German tourists find it. It was bizarre to be so close to the Mexican border and hear German spoken around me at dinner; and to watch a pack of desert dogs roaming unleashed past a wall painted with an Octoberfest-style mural. After an evening in the restaurant and bar, you'll know pretty much everyone in town. I overheard one long-time local saying, "When I first came to Jacumba, I couldn't stand the place. But it grows on you." That pretty much sums it up.

JACUMBA HOT SPRINGS SPA LODGE AND RESORT

Telephone. **(619) 766-4333; fax (619) 766-9017**
Address: **44500 Old Highway 80, P.O. Box 371, Jacumba 91934**
Rates: **$32 to $50**
Directions: **From I-80, forty-five miles east of San Diego, exit at Jacumba.**

LA QUINTA

La Quinta Resort

Built in 1926 as the first resort in the Palm Springs area, La Quinta Resort began with twenty Spanish-style casitas and has since grown to six hundred fifty rooms spread over forty-five acres. It doesn't look as big as it is. In fact, La Quinta has managed to keep its serene Spanish character largely intact. The long row of perfectly tapered cypress trees flanking the driveway, the conquistador statues at the main entry, the old tiles in the hacienda-style lobby, beautifully landscaped grounds, orange trees dripping with fruit—this is early Southern California.

The original, understated casitas—many named after various saints—still have the most character and are as popular as they were back in Hollywood's golden era when La Quinta was a retreat for celebrities. On their walls are Hollywood stars representing the movie people who have stayed here over the years. Ginger Rogers spent her honeymoon in No. 111, which has an old map of Mexico painted above the wood-burning fireplace, plus a screened-in lanai and porch swing. In 1934, Frank Capra wrote *It Happened One Night* in San Anselmo—now the most requested room—and wound up writing there every winter. Tucked far in the corner is La Casa, a private hacienda once leased to Greta Garbo and now used for private functions.

The grounds are wonderfully tranquil; the sound of birds is everywhere and the Santa Rosa Mountains offer a protective barrier from the wind. As you stroll around the original casitas, you'll find every plant indigenous to the Southern California desert represented. The entrance is splashed with a riot of colorful flowers. I also loved the nice touches in the lobby and lounge—a big bowl of apples at the front desk, the old-fashioned phones, afternoon tea, and not just one, but three fireplaces.

There's no lack of things to do here—twenty-five swimming pools, thirty-eight hot spas, thirty of the world's finest tennis courts, mountain golfing, and a fitness center. By the way, the seventeenth hole of the Dunes Course was selected by the PGA as one of the eighteen toughest golf holes in America.

LA QUINTA RESORT

Telephone: **(800) 598-3828; (619) 564-4111; fax (619) 564-5758**
Address: **49-499 Eisenhower Drive, P.O. Box 69, La Quinta 92253**
Rates: **$140 to $365 for rooms; $220 to $2600 for suites**
Directions: **nineteen miles southeast of Palm Springs; from I-10 (or SR-111 east), exit at Washington Street and turn right; proceed south to La Quinta and turn right at Eisenhower Drive.**

PALM DESERT

LITTLE NOVELTY: From the man-made lake in the atrium lobby of **Marriott's Desert Springs,** you can ride a little boat to one of the hotel's several restaurants. The big convention-oriented hotel also offers extensive services in their spa, including Ayurvedic treatments (an ancient healing science originating in India), thalassotherapy (seaweed) baths, and a Learn the Art of Massage session you can take with your partner. For more information, call (800) 331-3112 or (619) 341-2211.

PALM SPRINGS

Sakura Japanese Bed & Breakfast Inn

As the only Japanese-style bed and breakfast in this country, it's curious that Sakura exists in Palm Springs, of all places. This small, three–room inn is run by George Cebra, an American, and his Japanese wife, Fumiko. A professional jazz musician, George

The Sakura is a three-room inn that is the only Japanese-style bed & breakfast in the U.S.

spent two years working in the civilized clockwork of Japan and returned to find life in Los Angeles abrasive. He and Fumiko retreated to the desert. He still performs locally, while Fumiko leads Japanese tourists on golf tours of Palm Springs. George says most of the Japanese visitors prefer to stay in western-style hotels, but they often come to Sakura for the Japanese-style breakfasts.

Except for the ubiquitous Palm Springs bean-shaped swimming pool, the outside of the inn is fairly Japanese, with a blue-tiled roof, rock-and-Buddha garden, and bamboo screens. If you stay here, request the one guest room that is most traditionally Japanese. It has tatami mats and a futon on the floor, shoji screen windows, another futon couch, and low table (with a bowl of Korean ginseng candies) in the sitting area, Japanese artwork, and antique kimonos hanging on the walls. A kimono robe is folded neatly on top of the handmade futon quilt.

The only drawback at Sakura is the sound of the traffic whizzing by outside. But if you ask George to put on some Japanese music, the delicate koto and bamboo wood flute will nicely mask outside noise and enhance the soothing effect of the decor.

In the morning you can choose either an American or Japanese-style breakfast, which usually includes green tea, white rice, miso soup, and perhaps a little seaweed and crab. Upon request, Fumiko will sometimes cook dinners for the guests. A Japanese bathhouse is in the works, and shiatsu treatments are also available.

SAKURA JAPANESE BED & BREAKFAST INN

Telephone: **(800) 200-0705; (619) 327-0705; fax (619) 327-6847**
Address: **1677 North Via Miraleste, Palm Springs 92262**
Rates: **$45 to $65, including American or Japanese breakfast**
Directions: **From SR-111 south, turn left at Vista Chino and head east for three blocks. Look for the blue-tiled roof on the right.**

Korakia Pensione

With its hip, Mediterranean exotica, Korakia Pensione is an exciting departure from the traditional bed and breakfast. Built in 1924 by a Scottish painter who spent a lot of time in Tangiers, the

Korakia Pensione was a popular twenties rendezvous spot for artists and writers.

whitewashed villa was a popular gathering spot for artists and writers of the twenties. Now the newly restored inn is a hot getaway for celebrities such as Peter Coyote and Ted Danson.

Its castle-like turrets, Moorish archways, and light, airy spaces have an authentic feel of the Mediterranean—not quite one particular country, but rather a melange. In the courtyards featuring Moroccan bird cages and fountains, I felt like I could be in Spain or North Africa. But up in the Artist Studio (where Winston Churchill once painted), the whitewashed walls and simple muslin curtains reminded me of Greece. In the Library—another favorite guest room—the red-tiled floors are laid with Turkish carpets, the shelves are filled with rare books, and four-poster beds are piled with pillows made of deep, dark Middle Eastern fabrics. All of the styles blend wonderfully. It's no wonder *Vogue* and other high-profile magazines have already sniffed out Korakia—this place is a photographer's dream come true.

Doug Smith, the owner and restorer of the inn, looks more like a surfer than an architectural preservationist. Blond, tan, and talkative (I gave up trying to take notes), he sets an informal tone at Korakia. "This is very much Faulty Towers West," he says, meaning there are no pretensions and very few rules. Guests are free to use the communal kitchen, and sometimes there are impromptu dinners under the stars out by the swimming pool. Except for the San Jacinto Mountains looming behind Korakia, you'd never know you were in Palm Springs.

KORAKIA PENSIONE

Telephone: **(619) 864-6411**
Address: **257 South Patencio Road, Palm Springs 92262**
Rates: **$79 to $169, including continental breakfast; closed in August**
Directions: **From SR-111 (Palm Canyon Drive) south, turn right on Arenas Road, then left on Patencio Road.**

Spa Hotel & Casino

The only hotel that offers a casino in all of California is the Spa Hotel & Casino in downtown Palm Springs. Because it's owned by the Agua Caliente tribe of Cahuilla Indians, there are legal slot machines, blackjack, poker—the works. I visited here just after they opened, and the casino was packed. The hotel offers spa facilities with natural mineral springs. As for the rest of the hotel, the plain concrete facade and minimally landscaped grounds are uninspired.

SPA HOTEL & CASINO

Telephone: **(800) 854-1279; (619) 325-1461; fax (619) 325-3344**
Address: **100 North Indian Canyon Drive, Palm Springs 92262**
Rates: **$124 to $189**
Directions: **In downtown Palm Springs, on the corner of Indian Avenue and Tahquitz Way.**

Villa Royale

At the Villa Royale you can visit just about any country in Europe, depending on the room you book. Owners Bob Lee and Chuck Murawski—both avid travelers—have decorated each guest room and suite in a different international theme. The English Room, for instance, is pretty and flowery, filled with decor and Victorian antiques. The Italiano Room features marble floors, column-flanked doorways, and walls rag-washed for an ancient patina effect. Some of the motifs are fairly obscure, with little more than a poster of the chosen destination on the wall. Nonetheless, the European ambiance is strong enough to set this inn apart from most of the other institutional hotels in Palm Springs.

The maze of brick, bougainvillea-filled pathways that meander among the three guest buildings and swimming pools are quite lovely, with fountains, hanging flower pots, and gardens everywhere. Villa Royale also has a bar (an antique from Paris) and restaurant rated as one of best in the area.

VILLA ROYALE

Telephone: **(800) 245-2314; (619) 327-2314; fax (619) 322-3794**
Address: **1620 Indian Trail, Palm Springs 92264**
Rates: **$99 to $225, including continental breakfast**
Directions: **From SR-111 south (just after the big bend in downtown Palm Springs), turn left on Indian Trail.**

Le Petit Chateau

Palm Springs has more naturist resorts than any other area in California. Most have a strict policy: You must be completely unclothed when you're in the public areas. This way, everyone is in the same boat, so to speak.

If you've ever contemplated staying at a naturist place but aren't sure how comfortable you'd feel, Le Petit Chateau is a good place to start. A small, private, tasteful inn, it's the only clothing-optional bed and breakfast in the country. Says innkeeper Mary Robidoux, "Everyone comes for the nude sunbathing, but we don't have any rule that (says) you have to be unclothed around the pool."

Ten guest rooms, some with kitchens, are centered around a small swimming pool area brightly colored with bougainvillea and hibiscus. (A misting system cools the air on hot, dry days.) Classical music plays in the wicker-filled, open-air lounge where a breakfast buffet is served each morning, and hors d'oeuvres in the afternoon.

The inn draws both old and young well-traveled adults, most of whom just want to relax and be pampered by the sun. It's a safe, private environment—no big deal about the nudity. "We're very low-key," Mary says. "We're not out to change the world."

LE PETIT CHATEAU

Telephone:	**(619) 325-2686; fax (619) 322-5054**
Address:	**491 Via Soledad, Palm Springs 92264**
Rates:	**$80 to $130, including buffet breakfast**
Directions:	**Call for directions.**

Desert Shadows

If you want to go one step farther than Le Petit Chateau to a full-scale naturist resort, Desert Shadows is a comfortable place for first-timers. It's a pleasant, professionally run, full-service resort that welcomes families, children, singles, couples—absolutely anyone. The well-manicured grounds contain two swimming pools, tennis courts, volleyball, a workout room, and game room. You must be unclothed around the pool area.

Having never been to a naturist resort, I wasn't quite sure what to expect when I dropped by for a tour. Co-owner Stephen Payne greeted me at the reception desk and showed me around. Like some of the other guests, he was wearing a T-shirt, but nothing else. I consciously looked him in the eye the whole time we were talking. I was quite aware I was the only fully clothed person there besides the maids. It's more comfortable at a place like this to just take your clothes off and be done with it, like everyone else. As my few nudist friends love saying, "It's a great equalizer."

Stephen says they get a lot of first-timers, and after an initial ten minutes of uneasiness, the guests usually say, "What's the big deal?" It's not a sexy atmosphere when absolutely nothing is left to the imagination. And let's face it—most people are not that attractive when they're completely unclothed.

Stephen pointed out that guests who come here don't label themselves as nudists: "It's the one activity that everyone is imminently qualified for."

DESERT SHADOWS

Telephone: **(800) 292-9298; (619) 325-6410**
Address: **1533 Chaparral Road, Palm Springs 92262**
Rates: **$100 to $135, including continental breakfast; children under 12 free**
Directions: **Call for directions.**

DEATH VALLEY

Amargosa Opera House and Hotel

I wondered if it was a case of heat stroke when I first saw the Amargosa Opera House rising out of the desert on my way to Death Valley. It was a mere 110 degrees—I hadn't even reached the hottest stretch and already I was seeing mirages. Here in the middle of nowhere, at a junction so small you'd miss it if you blinked twice, was an opera house and hotel.

For twenty-seven years, every May to October, owner-dancer-painter Marta Becket has been giving one-woman performances of ballet and pantomime at Amargosa. The theater walls and domed ceiling are covered with murals of faux audiences—sixteenth-century Spanish royalty, clerics, gypsies, and revelers—which Marta painted.

The hotel itself—a long, low slab building—is hardly worth mentioning if it weren't for the adjacent opera house. Except for skylights in the bathrooms and various trompe l'oeil murals (again, painted by the busy Marta), the guest rooms are basic, spartan, and a bit rough around the edges. If she spruced up the rooms and added a swimming pool and restaurant, the hotel might show some promise. For now, the opera house is the main draw.

AMARGOSA OPERA HOUSE AND HOTEL

Telephone:	**(619) 852-4441; fax (619) 852-4138**
Address:	**P.O. Box 8, Death Valley Junction 92328**
Rates:	**$25 to $44**
Directions:	**on SR-127, in Death Valley Junction, thirty miles south of Furnace Creek.**

Furnace Creek Inn and Ranch Resort

Together, the Furnace Creek Inn and accompanying Ranch have the dubious distinction of being situated in the hottest, driest spot in the world, at one of the lowest elevations in California. I can vouch for the heat—I visited Death Valley in the summer when it was 115 degrees, and the locals were marveling about the cool spell. It feels like most of the heat is rising up out of the ground—that's because the ground temperature is usually 50 percent higher than the air temperature.

Of the three places to stay in Death Valley National Monument, the Furnace Creek Inn is the most luxurious. Built in 1927 by the Pacific Coast Borax Company, the hotel sits on a bluff overlooking the barren, lunar-like landscape of Death Valley. The palm-shaded, terraced grounds include lighted tennis courts, an archery range, exercise room, swimming pool, and, strangely, a sauna. Their eighteen-hole golf course (where the elevation makes golf balls fly farther) is a short drive down the road at Furnace Creek Ranch.

The Furnace Creek Ranch is much more, dare I say, down to earth than its rich sister up the road. Once the crew quarters for the Borax Company, Furnace Creek's spacious grounds, which are at a record elevation of 178 feet below sea level, contain more than two hundred informal motel and cabin units. (This is where all the tour groups stay.) It's also the only hotel in the world (thank goodness) with a borax museum—a barnlike structure consisting mostly of old mining machinery. With a palm-studded golf course surrounding it, the Ranch actually seems more oasis-like than the Inn. The guest units, unfortunately, are nothing special. If you do stay here, I'd recommend the motel rooms over the rather dreary-looking cabins.

FURNACE CREEK INN AND RANCH RESORT

Telephone: **(619) 786-2345; fax (619) 786-2307**
Address: **P.O. Box 1, Death Valley 92328**
Inn rates: **$275 to $375, including breakfast and dinner (closed from May to October)**
Ranch rates: **$70 to $120**
Directions: **on SR-190, in Death Valley National Monument.**

Stovepipe Wells Village

I was astonished when I called the Furnace Creek Ranch for a reservation in August—they were booked solid. Apparently, Europeans love visiting Death Valley in July and August. When you're coming from a country such as Germany where it's damp and overcast all the time, the hotter, the better.

So, my girlfriend and I wound up at Stovepipe Wells Village. After reading that some of the rooms didn't even have drinking water, we expected a dismal place. On the contrary, it was actually quite respectable, with a great view of Death Valley's most photogenic sand dunes. There's a restaurant (with beef as the main course every night), a friendly saloon, gift shop, market (complete with kipper snacks for the British tourists), and swimming pool. The guest rooms are quite acceptable, and from the Road Runner building you have an unobstructed view of the whole valley. As for the water, it's not actually poisonous, but so full of minerals it might upset your stomach. Some rooms have filtered water taps in the rooms; others offer drinking water just outside the rooms.

Stovepipe Wells has an authentic, rustic character that best captures what Death Valley is all about—something I didn't feel as much at Furnace Creek Inn and Ranch. It's craggy and rustic, not a palm tree in sight, and it fits in perfectly with its desolate surroundings.

But what I remember most about Stovepipe Wells was sitting outside late at night, watching a bevy of bats fly around the swimming pool. As my girlfriend and I dangled our legs in the water, the bats took turns touching the surface, then resumed their haphazard, circular flight.

STOVEPIPE WELLS VILLAGE

Telephone: **(619) 786-2387; (619) 786-2345**
Address: **Death Valley 92328**
Rates: **$53 to $80**
Directions: **on SR 190, in Stovepipe Wells.**

Lodgings Index

Offbeat Interest Index

Offbeat Overnights author Lucy Poshek, a well-traveled author and photographer, has written five other travel guides, including *Frommer's California Bed and Breakfast Guide* and *Frommer's Caribbean Bed and Breakfast Guide*. Poshek's travel trade experience includes four years' managing a California bed and breakfast inn, and six years as a travel counselor with the Automobile Club of Southern California. Poshek lives in Laguna Beach, California.